Amazon Kinesis Video Streams Developer Guide

A catalogue record for this book is available from the Hong Kong Public Libraries.

Published in Hong Kong by Samurai Media Limited.

Email: info@samuraimedia.org

ISBN 9789888407842

Contents

What Is Amazon Kinesis Video Streams?

Amazon Kinesis Video Streams is a fully managed AWS service that you can use to stream live video from devices to the AWS Cloud, or build applications for real-time video processing or batch-oriented video analytics.

Kinesis Video Streams isn't just storage for video data. You can use it to watch your video streams in real time as they are received in the cloud. You can either monitor your live streams in the AWS Management Console, or develop your own monitoring application that uses the Kinesis Video Streams API library to display live video.

You can use Kinesis Video Streams to capture massive amounts of live video data from millions of sources, including smartphones, security cameras, webcams, cameras embedded in cars, drones, and other sources. You can also send non-video time-serialized data such as audio data, thermal imagery, depth data, RADAR data, and more. As live video streams from these sources into a Kinesis video stream, you can build applications that can access the data, frame-by-frame, in real time for low-latency processing. Kinesis Video Streams is source-agnostic; you can stream video from a computer's webcam using the GStreamer library, or from a camera on your network using RTSP.

You can also configure your Kinesis video stream to durably store media data for the specified retention period. Kinesis Video Streams automatically stores this data and encrypts it at rest. Additionally, Kinesis Video Streams time-indexes stored data based on both the producer time stamps and ingestion time stamps. You can build applications that periodically batch-process the video data, or you can create applications that require ad hoc access to historical data for different use cases.

Your custom applications, real-time or batch-oriented, can run on Amazon EC2 instances. These applications might process data using open source deep-learning algorithms, or use third-party applications that integrate with Kinesis Video Streams.

Benefits of using Kinesis Video Streams include the following:

- **Connect and stream from millions of devices ** – Kinesis Video Streams enables you to connect and stream video, audio, and other data from millions of devices ranging from consumer smartphones, drones, dash cams, and more. You can use the Kinesis Video Streams producer libraries to configure your devices and reliably stream in real time, or as after-the-fact media uploads.
- **Durably store, encrypt, and index data **– You can configure your Kinesis video stream to durably store media data for custom retention periods. Kinesis Video Streams also generates an index over the stored data based on producer-generated or service-side time stamps. Your applications can easily retrieve specified data in a stream using the time-index.
- **Focus on managing applications instead of infrastructure** – Kinesis Video Streams is serverless, so there is no infrastructure to set up or manage. You don't need to worry about the deployment, configuration, or elastic scaling of the underlying infrastructure as your data streams and number of consuming applications grow and shrink. Kinesis Video Streams automatically does all the administration and maintenance required to manage streams, so you can focus on the applications, not the infrastructure.
- **Build real-time and batch applications on data streams** – You can use Kinesis Video Streams to build custom real-time applications that operate on live data streams, and create batch or ad hoc applications that operate on durably persisted data without strict latency requirements. You can build, deploy, and manage custom applications: open source (Apache MXNet, OpenCV), homegrown, or third-party solutions via the AWS Marketplace to process and analyze your streams. Kinesis Video Streams `Get` APIs enable you to build multiple concurrent applications processing data in a real-time or batch-oriented basis.
- **Stream data more securely ** – Kinesis Video Streams encrypts all data as it flows through the service and when it persists the data. Kinesis Video Streams enforces Transport Layer Security (TLS)-based encryption on data streaming from devices, and encrypts all data at rest using AWS Key Management Service (AWS KMS). Additionally, you can manage access to your data using AWS Identity and Access Management (IAM).
- **Pay as you go ** – For more information, see AWS Pricing.

Kinesis Video Streams is suitable for a variety of industry scenarios. For example:

- Smart city initiatives – Push video streams from traffic cameras to Kinesis video streams, and write consumer applications that can track real-time traffic patterns. You can also batch process the historical data to understand changes that result from new construction or traffic routing changes.
- Home scenarios – Connect home security cameras, baby monitors, and other cameras embedded in appliances to build experiences that keep consumers safe and make their lives more productive and fun.
- Intelligent retail features – Capture video from multiple in-store cameras to automate people-counting, generate store heat maps to understand in-store customer activity, optimize layout and merchandise display, and other actions to help drive customer satisfaction.
- Industrial automation – Use license plate readers that automatically detect when trucks enter and leave the warehouse. Count pallets and track movement of material and goods on the shop floor. Use thermal cameras to notify when industrial machinery is overheating to drive preventative maintenance and keep workers safe.

Are You a First-Time User of Kinesis Video Streams?

If you're a first-time user of Kinesis Video Streams, we recommend that you read the following sections in order:

1. **Amazon Kinesis Video Streams: How It Works** – To learn about Kinesis Video Streams concepts.

2. **Getting Started with Kinesis Video Streams** – To set up your account and test Kinesis Video Streams.

3. **Kinesis Video Streams Producer Libraries** – To learn about creating a Kinesis Video Streams producer application.

4. **Kinesis Video Stream Parser Library** – To learn about processing incoming data frames in a Kinesis Video Streams consumer application.

5. **Amazon Kinesis Video Streams Examples** – To see more examples of what you can do with Kinesis Video Streams.

Kinesis Video Streams System Requirements

The following sections contain hardware, software, and storage requirements for Amazon Kinesis Video Streams.

Topics

- Camera Requirements
- SDK Storage Requirements

Camera Requirements

Cameras that are used for running the Kinesis Video Streams Producer SDK and samples have the following memory requirements:

- The SDK content view requires 16 MB of memory.
- The sample application default configuration is 512 MB. This value is appropriate for producers that have good network connectivity and no requirements for additional buffering. If the network connectivity is poor and more buffering is required, you can calculate the memory requirement per second of buffering by multiplying the frame rate per second by the frame memory size. For more information about allocating memory, see StorageInfo.

We recommend using USB or RTSP (Real Time Streaming Protocol) cameras that encode data using H.264 because this removes the encoding workload from the CPU.

Currently, the demo application does not support the User Datagram Protocol (UDP) for RTSP streaming. This capability will be added in the future.

The Producer SDK supports the following types of cameras:

- Web cameras.
- USB cameras.
- Cameras with H.264 encoding (preferred).
- Cameras without H.264 encoding.
- Raspberry Pi camera module. This is preferred for Raspberry Pi devices because it connects to the GPU for video data transfer, so there is no overhead for CPU processing.
- RTSP (network) cameras. These cameras are preferred because the video streams are already encoded with H.264.

Tested Cameras

We have tested the following USB cameras with Kinesis Video Streams:

- Logitech 1080p
- Logitech C930
- Logitech C920 (H.264)
- Logitech Brio (4K)
- SVPRO USB Camera 170degree Fisheye Lens Wide Angle 1080P 2mp Sony IMX322 HD H.264 30fps Mini Aluminum USB Webcam Camera

We have tested the following IP cameras with Kinesis Video Streams:

- Vivotek FD9371 – HTV/EHTV
- Vivotek IB9371 – HT
- Hikvision 3MP IP Camera DS-2CD2035FWD-I
- Sricam SP012 IP
- VStarcam 720P WiFi IP Camera (TCP)
- Ipccam Security Surveillance IP Camera 1080P

- AXIS P3354 Fixed Dome Network Camera

Of the cameras that were tested with Kinesis Video Streams, the Vivotek cameras have the most consistent RTSP stream. The Sricam camera has the least consistent RTSP stream.

Tested Operating Systems

We have tested web cameras and RTSP cameras with the following devices and operating systems:

- Mac mini
  - High Sierra
- MacBook Pro laptops
  - Sierra (10.12)
  - El Capitan (10.11)
- HP laptops running Ubuntu 16.04
- Ubuntu 17.10 (Docker container)
- Raspberry Pi 3

SDK Storage Requirements

Installing the Kinesis Video Streams Producer Libraries has a minimum storage requirement of 170 MB and a recommended storage requirement of 512 MB.

Amazon Kinesis Video Streams: How It Works

Topics

- Kinesis Video Streams API and Producer Libraries Support
- Controlling Access to Kinesis Video Streams Resources Using IAM
- Using Server-Side Encryption with Kinesis Video Streams
- Kinesis Video Streams Data Model

Amazon Kinesis Video Streams is a fully managed AWS service that enables you to stream live video from devices to the AWS Cloud and durably store it. You can then build your own applications for real-time video processing or perform batch-oriented video analytics.

The following diagram provides an overview of how Kinesis Video Streams works.

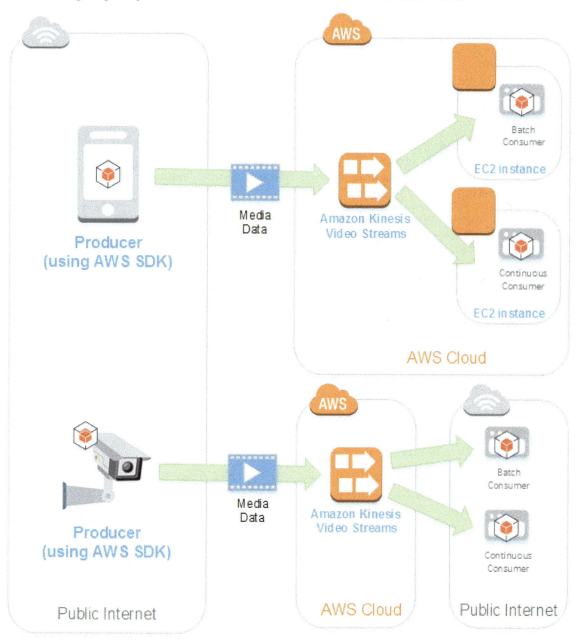

The diagram demonstrates the interaction among the following components:

- **Producer** – Any source that puts data into a Kinesis video stream. A producer can be any video-generating device, such as a security camera, a body-worn camera, a smartphone camera, or a dashboard camera. A producer can also send non-video data, such as audio feeds, images, or RADAR data.

  A single producer can generate one or more video streams. For example, a video camera can push video data to one Kinesis video stream and audio data to another.

  - **Kinesis Video Streams Producer libraries** – A set of easy-to-use software and libraries that you can install and configure on your devices. These libraries make it easy to securely connect and reliably stream video in different ways, including in real time, after buffering it for a few seconds, or as after-the-fact media uploads.

- **Kinesis video stream** – A resource that enables you to transport live video data, optionally store it, and make the data available for consumption both in real time and on a batch or ad hoc basis. In a typical configuration, a Kinesis video stream has only one producer publishing data into it.

  The stream can carry audio, video, and similar time-encoded data streams, such as depth sensing feeds, RADAR feeds, and more. You create a Kinesis video stream using the AWS Management Console or programmatically using the AWS SDKs.

  Multiple independent applications can consume a Kinesis video stream in parallel.

- **Consumer** – Gets data, such as fragments and frames, from a Kinesis video stream to view, process, or analyze it. Generally these consumers are called Kinesis Video Streams applications. You can write applications that consume and process data in Kinesis video streams in real time, or after the data is durably stored and time-indexed when low latency processing is not required. You can create these consumer applications to run on Amazon EC2 instances.

  - Kinesis Video Stream Parser Library – Enables Kinesis Video Streams applications to reliably get media from Kinesis video streams in a low-latency manner. Additionally, it parses the frame boundaries in the media so that applications can focus on processing and analyzing the frames themselves.

Kinesis Video Streams API and Producer Libraries Support

Kinesis Video Streams provides APIs for you to create and manage streams and read or write media data to and from a stream. The Kinesis Video Streams console, in addition to administration functionality, also supports live and video-on-demand playback. Kinesis Video Streams also provides a set of producer libraries that you can use in your application code to extract data from your media sources and upload to your Kinesis video stream.

Topics

- Kinesis Video Streams API
- Producer Libraries

Kinesis Video Streams API

Kinesis Video Streams provides APIs for creating and managing Kinesis video streams. It also provides APIs for reading and writing media data to a stream, as follows:

- **Producer API** – Kinesis Video Streams provides a `PutMedia` API to write media data to a Kinesis video stream. In a `PutMedia` request, the producer sends a stream of media fragments. A *fragment* is a self-contained sequence of frames. The frames belonging to a fragment should have no dependency on any frames from other fragments. For more information, see PutMedia.

  As fragments arrive, Kinesis Video Streams assigns a unique fragment number, in increasing order. It also stores producer-side and server-side time stamps for each fragment, as Kinesis Video Streams-specific metadata.

- **Consumer APIs** –The following APIs enable consumers to get data from a stream:

  - `GetMedia` - When using this API, consumers must identify the starting fragment. The API then returns fragments in the order in which they were added to the stream (in increasing order by fragment number). The media data in the fragments is packed into a structured format such as Matroska (MKV). For more information, see GetMedia. **Note**
    `GetMedia` knows where the fragments are (archived in the data store or available in real time). For example, if `GetMedia` determines that the starting fragment is archived, it starts returning fragments from the data store. When it needs to return newer fragments that are not archived yet, `GetMedia` switches to reading fragments from an in-memory stream buffer.

    This is an example of a continuous consumer, which processes fragments in the order that they are ingested by the stream.

    `GetMedia` enables video-processing applications to fail or fall behind, and then catch up with no additional effort. Using `GetMedia`, applications can process data that's archived in the data store, and as the application catches up, `GetMedia` continues to feed media data in real time as it arrives.

  - `GetMediaFromFragmentList` (and `ListFragments`) - Batch processing applications are considered offline consumers. Offline consumers might choose to explicitly fetch particular media fragments or ranges of video by combining the `ListFragments` and `GetMediaFromFragmentList` APIs. `ListFragments` and `GetMediaFromFragmentList` enable an application to identify segments of video for a particular time range or fragment range, and then fetch those fragments either sequentially or in parallel for processing. This approach is suitable for `MapReduce` application suites, which must quickly process large amounts of data in parallel.

    For example, suppose that a consumer wants to process one day's worth of video fragments. The consumer would do the following:

    1. Get a list of fragments by calling the `ListFragments` API and specifying a time range to select the desired collection of fragments.

The API returns metadata from all the fragments in the specified time range. The metadata provides information such as fragment number, producer-side/server-side time stamps, and so on.

2. Take the fragment metadata list and retrieve fragments, in any order. For example, to process all the fragments for the day, the consumer might choose to split the list into sub-lists and have workers (for example, multiple Amazon EC2 instances) fetch the fragments in parallel using the `GetMediaFromFragmentList`, and process them in parallel.

The following diagram shows the data flow for fragments and chunks during these API calls.

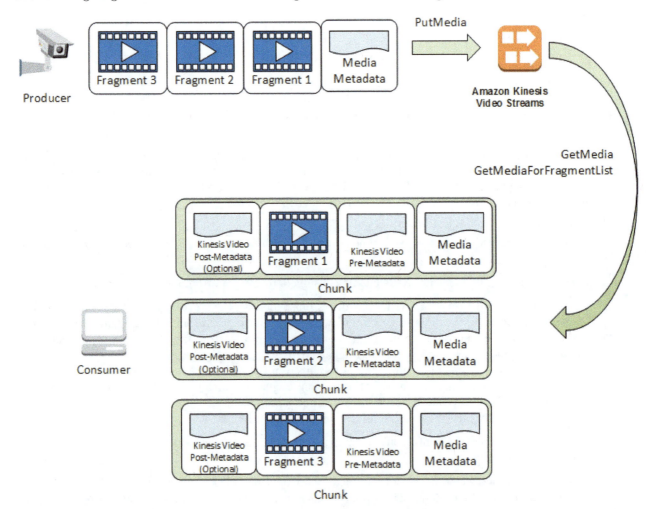

When a producer sends a `PutMedia` request, it sends media metadata in the payload, and then sends a sequence of media data fragments. Upon receiving the data, Kinesis Video Streams stores incoming media data as Kinesis Video Streams chunks. Each chunk consists of the following:

- A copy of the media metadata
- A fragment
- Kinesis Video Streams-specific metadata; for example, the fragment number and server-side and producer-side time stamps

When a consumer requests media metadata, Kinesis Video Streams returns a stream of chunks, starting with the fragment number that you specify in the request.

If you enable data persistence for the stream, after receiving a fragment on the stream, Kinesis Video Streams also saves a copy of the fragment to the data store.

Producer Libraries

After you create a Kinesis video stream, you can start sending data to the stream. In your application code, you can use these libraries to extract data from your media sources and upload to your Kinesis video stream. For more information about the available producer libraries, see Kinesis Video Streams Producer Libraries.

Controlling Access to Kinesis Video Streams Resources Using IAM

By using AWS Identity and Access Management (IAM) with Amazon Kinesis Video Streams, you can control whether users in your organization can perform a task using specific Kinesis Video Streams API operations and whether they can use specific AWS resources.

For more information about IAM, see the following:

- AWS Identity and Access Management (IAM)
- Getting Started
- IAM User Guide

Topics

- Policy Syntax
- Actions for Kinesis Video Streams
- Amazon Resource Names (ARNs) for Kinesis Video Streams
- Granting Other IAM Accounts Access to a Kinesis Video Stream
- Example Policies for Kinesis Video Streams

Policy Syntax

An IAM policy is a JSON document that consists of one or more statements. Each statement is structured as follows:

```
1  {
2    "Statement":[{
3      "Effect":"effect",
4      "Action":"action",
5      "Resource":"arn",
6      "Condition":{
7        "condition":{
8          "key":"value"
9          }
10        }
11      }
12    ]
13  }
```

There are various elements that make up a statement:

- **Effect:** The *effect* can be `Allow` or `Deny`. By default, IAM users don't have permission to use resources and API actions, so all requests are denied. An explicit allow overrides the default. An explicit deny overrides any allows.
- **Action:** The *action* is the specific API action for which you are granting or denying permission.
- **Resource:** The resource that's affected by the action. To specify a resource in the statement, you need to use its Amazon Resource Name (ARN).
- **Condition:** Conditions are optional. They can be used to control when your policy is in effect.

As you create and manage IAM policies, you might want to use the IAM Policy Generator and the IAM Policy Simulator.

Actions for Kinesis Video Streams

In an IAM policy statement, you can specify any API action from any service that supports IAM. For Kinesis Video Streams, use the following prefix with the name of the API action: `kinesisvideo:`. For example:

`kinesisvideo:CreateStream`, `kinesisvideo:ListStreams`, and `kinesisvideo:DescribeStream`.

To specify multiple actions in a single statement, separate them with commas as follows:

```
1  "Action": ["kinesisvideo:action1", "kinesisvideo:action2"]
```

You can also specify multiple actions using wildcards. For example, you can specify all actions whose name begins with the word "Get" as follows:

```
1  "Action": "kinesisvideo:Get*"
```

To specify all Kinesis Video Streams operations, use the asterisk (*) wildcard as follows:

```
1  "Action": "kinesisvideo:*"
```

For the complete list of Kinesis Video Streams API actions, see the http://docs.aws.amazon.com/kinesisvideostreams/latest/dg/API_Reference.html.

Amazon Resource Names (ARNs) for Kinesis Video Streams

Each IAM policy statement applies to the resources that you specify using their ARNs.

Use the following ARN resource format for Kinesis Video Streams:

```
1  arn:aws:kinesisvideo:region:account-id:stream/stream-name/code
```

For example:

```
1  "Resource": arn:aws:kinesisvideo::*:111122223333:stream/my-stream/0123456789012
```

You can get the ARN of a stream using DescribeStream.

Granting Other IAM Accounts Access to a Kinesis Video Stream

You might need to grant permission to other IAM accounts to perform operations on Kinesis video streams. The following overview describes the general steps to grant access to video streams across accounts:

1. Get the 12-digit account ID of the account that you want to grant permissions to perform operations on your stream (for example, 111111111111).

2. Create a managed policy on the account that owns the stream that allows the level of access that you want to grant. For example policies for Kinesis Video Streams resources, see Example Policies in the next section.

3. Create a role, specifying the account to which you are granting permissions, and attach the policy that you created in the previous step.

4. Create a managed policy that allows the `AssumeRole` action on the role you created in the previous step. For example, the role might look like the following:

```
1  {
2    "Version": "2012-10-17",
3    "Statement": {
4      "Effect": "Allow",
5      "Action": "sts:AssumeRole",
6      "Resource": "arn:aws:iam::123456789012:role/CustomRole"
7    }
8  }
```

For step-by-step instructions on granting cross-account access, see Delegate Access Across AWS Accounts Using IAM Roles.

Example Policies for Kinesis Video Streams

The following example policies demonstrate how you can control user access to your Kinesis video streams.

Example 1: Allow users to get data from any Kinesis video stream
This policy allows a user or group to perform the DescribeStream, GetDataEndpoint, GetMedia, ListStreams, and ListTagsForStream operations on any Kinesis video stream. This policy is appropriate for users who can get data from any video stream.

```
1  {
2      "Version": "2012-10-17",
3      "Statement": [
4          {
5              "Effect": "Allow",
6              "Action": [
7                  "kinesisvideo:Describe*",
8                  "kinesisvideo:Get*",
9                  "kinesisvideo:List*"
10             ],
11             "Resource": "*"
12         }
13     ]
14 }
```

Example 2: Allow a user to create a Kinesis video stream and write data to it
This policy allows a user or group to perform the CreateStream and PutMedia operations. This policy is appropriate for a security camera that can create a video stream and send data to it.

```
1  {
2      "Statement": [
3          {
4              "Effect": "Allow",
5              "Action": [
6                  "kinesisvideo:CreateStream",
7                  "kinesisvideo:PutMedia"
8              ],
9              "Resource": "*"
10         }
11     ]
12 }
```

Example 3: Allow a user full access to all Kinesis Video Streams resources
This policy allows a user or group to perform any Kinesis Video Streams operation on any resource. This policy is appropriate for administrators.

```
1  {
2      "Version": "2012-10-17",
3      "Statement": [
4          {
5              "Effect": "Allow",
6              "Action": "kinesisvideo:*",
7              "Resource": "*"
8          }
9      ]
10 }
```

Example 4: Allow a user to write data to a specific Kinesis video stream

This policy allows a user or group to write data to a specific video stream. This policy is appropriate for a device that can send data to a single stream.

```
1  {
2      "Version": "2012-10-17",
3      "Statement": [
4          {
5              "Effect": "Allow",
6              "Action": "kinesisvideo:PutMedia",
7              "Resource": "arn:aws:kinesisvideo:us-west-2:123456789012:stream/your_stream
                   /0123456789012"
8          }
9      ]
10 }
```

Using Server-Side Encryption with Kinesis Video Streams

Server-side encryption using AWS Key Management Service (AWS KMS) keys makes it easier for you to meet strict data management requirements by encrypting your data at rest in Amazon Kinesis Video Streams.

Topics

- What Is Server-Side Encryption for Kinesis Video Streams?
- Costs, Regions, and Performance Considerations
- How Do I Get Started with Server-Side Encryption?
- Creating and Using User-Generated AWS KMS Master Keys
- Permissions to Use User-Generated AWS KMS Master Keys

What Is Server-Side Encryption for Kinesis Video Streams?

Server-side encryption is a feature in Kinesis Video Streams that automatically encrypts data before it's at rest by using an AWS KMS customer master key (CMK) that you specify. Data is encrypted before it is written to the Kinesis Video Streams stream storage layer, and it is decrypted after it is retrieved from storage. As a result, your data is always encrypted at rest within the Kinesis Video Streams service.

With server-side encryption, your Kinesis video stream producers and consumers don't need to manage master keys or cryptographic operations. If data retention is enabled, your data is automatically encrypted as it enters and leaves Kinesis Video Streams, so your data at rest is encrypted. AWS KMS provides all the master keys that are used by the server-side encryption feature. AWS KMS makes it easier to use a CMK for Kinesis Video Streams that is managed by AWS, a user-specified AWS KMS CMK, or a master key imported into the AWS KMS service.

Costs, Regions, and Performance Considerations

When you apply server-side encryption, you are subject to AWS KMS API usage and key costs. Unlike custom AWS KMS master keys, the `(Default) aws/kinesis-video` customer master key (CMK) is offered free of charge. However, you still must pay for the API usage costs that Kinesis Video Streams incurs on your behalf.

API usage costs apply for every CMK, including custom ones. The KMS costs scale with the number of user credentials that you use on your data producers and consumers because each user credential requires a unique API call to AWS KMS.

The following describes the costs by resource:

Keys

- The CMK for Kinesis Video Streams that's managed by AWS (alias = `aws/kinesis-video`) is free.
- User-generated AWS KMS keys are subject to AWS KMS key costs. For more information, see AWS Key Management Service Pricing.

AWS KMS API Usage

API requests to generate new data encryption keys or to retrieve existing encryption keys increase as traffic increases, and are subject to AWS KMS usage costs. For more information, see AWS Key Management Service Pricing: Usage.

Kinesis Video Streams generates key requests even when retention is set to 0 (no retention).

Availability of Server-Side Encryption by Region

Server-side encryption of Kinesis video streams is available in all the AWS Regions where Kinesis Video Streams is available.

How Do I Get Started with Server-Side Encryption?

Server-side encryption is always enabled on Kinesis video streams. If a user-provided key is not specified when the stream is created, the default key (provided by Kinesis Video Streams) is used.

A user-provided AWS KMS master key must be assigned to a Kinesis video stream when it is created. You can't later assign a different key to a stream using the UpdateStream API.

You can assign a user-provided AWS KMS master key to a Kinesis video stream in two ways:

- When creating a Kinesis video stream in the AWS Management Console, specify the AWS KMS master key in the **Encryption** section on the **Create new Kinesis Video stream** page.
- When creating a Kinesis video stream using the CreateStream API, specify the key ID in the `KmsKeyId` parameter.

Creating and Using User-Generated AWS KMS Master Keys

This section describes how to create and use your own AWS KMS master keys instead of using the master key administered by Amazon Kinesis Video Streams.

Creating User-Generated AWS KMS Master Keys

For information about how to create your own master keys, see Creating Keys in the *AWS Key Management Service Developer Guide*. After you create keys for your account, the Kinesis Video Streams service returns these keys in the **KMS master key** list.

Using User-Generated AWS KMS Master Keys

After the correct permissions are applied to your consumers, producers, and administrators, you can use custom AWS KMS master keys in your own AWS account or another AWS account. All AWS KMS master keys in your account appear in the **KMS Master Key** list on the console.

To use custom AWS KMS master keys that are located in another account, you must have permissions to use those keys. You must also create the stream using the `CreateStream` API. You can't use AWS KMS master keys from different accounts in streams created in the console.

Note
The AWS KMS key is not accessed until the `PutMedia` or `GetMedia` operation is executed. This has the following results:
If the key you specify doesn't exist, the `CreateStream` operation succeeds, but `PutMedia` and `GetMedia` operations on the stream fail. If you use the provided master key (`aws/kinesis-video`), the key is not present in your account until the first `PutMedia` or `GetMedia` operation is performed.

Permissions to Use User-Generated AWS KMS Master Keys

Before you can use server-side encryption with a user-generated AWS KMS master key, you must configure AWS KMS key policies to allow encryption of streams and encryption and decryption of stream records. For examples and more information about AWS KMS permissions, see AWS KMS API Permissions: Actions and Resources Reference.

Note

The use of the default service key for encryption does not require application of custom IAM permissions.

Before you use user-generated AWS KMS master keys, ensure that your Kinesis video stream producers and consumers (IAM principals) are users in the AWS KMS master key policy. Otherwise, writes and reads from a stream will fail, which could ultimately result in data loss, delayed processing, or hung applications. You can manage permissions for AWS KMS keys using IAM policies. For more information, see Using IAM Policies with AWS KMS.

Example Producer Permissions

Your Kinesis video stream producers must have the `kms:GenerateDataKey` permission:

```
 1 {
 2   "Version": "2012-10-17",
 3   "Statement": [
 4     {
 5         "Effect": "Allow",
 6         "Action": [
 7             "kms:GenerateDataKey"
 8         ],
 9         "Resource": "arn:aws:kms:us-west-2:123456789012:key/1234abcd-12ab-34cd-56ef-1234567890ab
             "
10     },
11     {
12         "Effect": "Allow",
13         "Action": [
14             "kinesis-video:PutMedia",
15         ],
16         "Resource": "arn:aws:kinesis-video:*:123456789012:MyStream"
17     }
18   ]
19 }
```

Example Consumer Permissions

Your Kinesis video stream consumers must have the `kms:Decrypt` permission:

```
 1 {
 2   "Version": "2012-10-17",
 3   "Statement": [
 4     {
 5         "Effect": "Allow",
 6         "Action": [
 7             "kms:Decrypt"
 8         ],
 9         "Resource": "arn:aws:kms:us-west-2:123456789012:key/1234abcd-12ab-34cd-56ef-1234567890ab
             "
10     },
11     {
12         "Effect": "Allow",
13         "Action": [
```

```
14            "kinesis-video:GetMedia",
15        ],
16        "Resource": "arn:aws:kinesis-video:*:123456789012:MyStream"
17    }
18  ]
19 }
```

Kinesis Video Streams Data Model

The Producer Libraries and Stream Parser Library send and receive video data in a format that supports embedding information alongside video data. This format is based on the Matroska (MKV) specification.

The MKV format is an open specification for media data. All the libraries and code examples in the *Amazon Kinesis Video Streams Developer Guide* send or receive data in the MKV format.

The Kinesis Video Streams Producer Libraries use the `StreamDefinition` and `Frame` types to produce MKV stream headers, frame headers, and frame data.

For information about the full MKV specification, see Matroska Specifications.

The following sections describe the components of MKV-formatted data produced by the C++ Producer Library.

Topics

- Stream Header Elements
- Frame Header Elements
- MKV Frame Data

Stream Header Elements

The following MKV header elements are used by `StreamDefinition` (defined in `StreamDefinition.h`).

Element	Description	Typical Values
stream_name	Corresponds to the name of the Kinesis video stream.	my-stream
retention_period	The duration that stream data is persisted by Kinesis Video Streams. Specify 0 for a stream that does not retain data.	24
tags	A key-value collection of user data. This data is displayed in the AWS Management Console and can be read by client applications to filter or get information about a stream.	
kms_key_id	If present, the user-defined AWS KMS master key that is used to encrypt data on the stream. If it is absent, the data is encrypted by the Kinesis-supplied master key (aws/kinesis-video).	01234567-89ab-cdef-0123-456789ab
streaming_type	Currently, the only valid streaming type is STREAMING_TYPE_REALTIME.	STREAMING_TYPE_REALTIME
content_type	The user-defined content type. For streaming video data to play in the console, the content type must be video/h264.	video/h264

Element	Description	Typical Values
max_latency	This value is not currently used and should be set to 0.	0
fragment_duration	The estimate of how long your fragments should be, which is used for optimization. The actual fragment duration is determined by the streaming data.	2
timecode_scale	Indicates the scale used by frame time stamps. The default is 1 millisecond. Specifying 0 also assigns the default value of 1 millisecond. This value can be between 100 nanoseconds and 1 second. For more information, see TimecodeScale in the Matroska documentation.	
key_frame_fragmentation	If true, the stream starts a new cluster when a keyframe is received.	true
frame_timecodes	If true, Kinesis Video Streams stamps the frames when they are received. If false, Kinesis Video Streams uses the decode time of the received frames.	true
absolute_fragment_time	If true, the cluster timecodes are interpreted as using absolute time (for example, from the producer's system clock). If false, the cluster timecodes are interpreted as being relative to the start time of the stream.	true
fragment_acks	If true, acknowledgements (ACKs) are sent when Kinesis Video Streams receives the data. The ACKs can be received using the KinesisVideoStreamFragmentAck or KinesisVideoStreamParseFragmentAck callbacks.	true
restart_on_error	Indicates whether the stream should resume transmission after a stream error is raised.	true

Element	Description	Typical Values
nal_adaptation_flags	Indicates whether NAL (Network Abstraction Layer) adaptation or codec private data is present in the content. Valid flags include NAL_ADAPTATION_ANNEXB_NALS and NAL_ADAPTATION_ANNEXB_CPD_NALS.	NAL_ADAPTATION_ANNEXB_NALS
frame_rate	An estimate of the content frame rate. This value is used for optimization; the actual frame rate is determined by the rate of incoming data. Specifying 0 assigns the default of 24.	24
avg_bandwith_bps	An estimate of the content bandwidth. This value is used for optimization; the actual rate is determined by the bandwidth of incoming data. For example, for a 720 p resolution video stream running at 25 FPS, you can expect the average bandwidth to be 5 Mbps.	5
buffer_duration	The duration that content is to be buffered on the producer. If there is low network latency, this value can be reduced; if network latency is high, increasing this value prevents frames from being dropped before they can be sent, due to allocation failing to put frames into the smaller buffer.	
replay_duration	The amount of time the video data stream is "rewound" in the case of connection loss. This value can be zero if lost frames due to connection loss are not a concern; the value can be increased if the consuming application can eliminate redundant frames. This value should be less than the buffer duration; otherwise the buffer duration is used.	
connection_staleness	The duration that a connection is maintained when no data is received.	

Element	Description	Typical Values
codec_id	The codec used by the content. For more information, see CodecID in the Matroska specification.	V_MPEG2
track_name	The user-defined name of the track.	my_track
codecPrivateData	Data provided by the encoder used to decode the frame data, such as the frame width and height in pixels, which is needed by many downstream consumers. In the C++ Producer Library, the gMkvTrackVideoBits array in MkvStatics.cpp includes pixel width and height for the frame.	
codecPrivateDataSize	The size of the data in the codecPrivateData parameter.	

Frame Header Elements

The following MKV header elements are used by `Frame` (defined in the `KinesisVideoPic` package, in `mkvgen/Include.h`):

- **Frame Index:** A monotonically increasing value.
- **Flags:** The type of frame. Valid values include the following:
  - `FRAME_FLAGS_NONE`
  - `FRAME_FLAG_KEY_FRAME`: If `key_frame_fragmentation` is set on the stream, key frames start a new fragment.
  - `FRAME_FLAG_DISCARDABLE_FRAME`: Tells the decoder that it can discard this frame if decoding is slow.
  - `FRAME_FLAG_INVISIBLE_FRAME`: Duration of this block is 0.
- **Decoding Timestamp:** The time stamp of when this frame was decoded. If previous frames depend on this frame for decoding, this time stamp might be earlier than that of earlier frames. This value is relative to the start of the fragment.
- **Presentation Timestamp:** The time stamp of when this frame is displayed. This value is relative to the start of the fragment.
- **Duration:** The playback duration of the frame.
- **Size:** The size of the frame data in bytes

MKV Frame Data

The data in `frame.frameData` might contain only media data for the frame, or it might contain further nested header information, depending on the encoding schema used. To be displayed in the AWS Management Console, the data must be encoded in the H.264 codec, but Kinesis Video Streams can receive time-serialized data streams in any format.

Getting Started with Kinesis Video Streams

This section describes how to perform the following tasks in Amazon Kinesis Video Streams:

- Set up your AWS account and create an administrator, if you haven't already done so.
- Create a Kinesis video stream.

Other sections in this guide describe how to send data to the stream and view data on the stream.

If you are new to Amazon Kinesis Video Streams, we recommend that you read Amazon Kinesis Video Streams: How It Works first.

Note
Following the Getting Started sample will not incur any charges to your AWS account. See Amazon Kinesis Video Streams Pricing for data costs in your region.

Topics

- Step 1: Set Up an AWS Account and Create an Administrator
- Step 2: Create a Kinesis Video Stream
- What's Next?

Step 1: Set Up an AWS Account and Create an Administrator

Before you use Kinesis Video Streams for the first time, complete the following tasks:

1. Sign Up for AWS (unless you already have an account)
2. Create an Administrator IAM User

Sign Up for AWS

If you already have an AWS account, you can skip this step.

When you sign up for Amazon Web Services (AWS), your AWS account is automatically signed up for all services in AWS, including Kinesis Video Streams. When you use Kinesis Video Streams, you are charged based on the amount of data ingested into, stored by, and consumed from the service. If you are a new AWS customer, you can get started with Kinesis Video Streams for free. For more information, see AWS Free Usage Tier.

To create an AWS account

1. Open https://aws.amazon.com/, and then choose **Create an AWS Account. Note**
   This might be unavailable in your browser if you previously signed into the AWS Management Console. In that case, choose **Sign in to a different account**, and then choose **Create a new AWS account**.

2. Follow the online instructions.

   Part of the sign-up procedure involves receiving a phone call and entering a PIN using the phone keypad.

Write down your AWS account ID because you need it for the next task.

Create an Administrator IAM User

When you sign up for AWS, you provide an email address and password that is associated with your AWS account. This is your *AWS account root user*. Its credentials provide complete access to all of your AWS resources.

Note
For security reasons, we recommend that you use the root user only to create an *administrator*, which is an *IAM user* with full permissions to your AWS account. You can then use this administrator to create other IAM users and roles with limited permissions. For more information, see IAM Best Practices and Creating an Admin User and Group in the *IAM User Guide*.

To create an administrator and sign into the console

1. Create an administrator in your AWS account. For instructions, see Creating Your First IAM User and Administrators Group in the *IAM User Guide*.

2. As an administrator, you can sign in to the console using a special URL. For more information, see How Users Sign in to Your Account in the *IAM User Guide*.

The administrator can create more users in the account. IAM users by default don't have any permissions. The administrator can create users and manage their permissions. For more information, see Creating Your First IAM User and Administrators Group.

For more information about IAM, see the following:

- AWS Identity and Access Management (IAM)
- Getting Started
- IAM User Guide

Next Step

Step 2: Create a Kinesis Video Stream

Step 2: Create a Kinesis Video Stream

This section describes how to create a Kinesis video stream.

This section contains the following procedures:

- Create a Video Stream Using the Console
- Create a Video Stream Using the AWS CLI

Create a Video Stream Using the Console

1. Sign in to the AWS Management Console and open the Kinesis console at https://console.aws.amazon.com/kinesis.

2. On the **Manage streams** page, choose **Create**.

3. On the **Create new KinesisVideo Stream** page, type **ExampleStream** for the stream name. Leave the **Use default settings** check box selected.

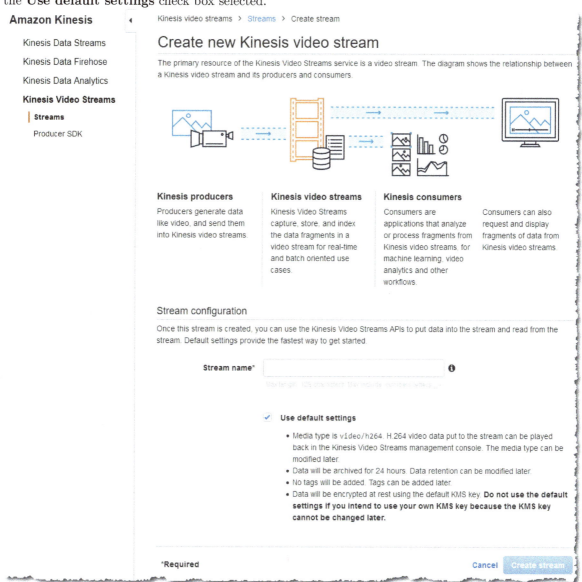

4. Choose **Create stream**.

5. After Kinesis Video Streams creates the stream, review the details on the **ExampleStream** page.

Create a Video Stream Using the AWS CLI

1. Ensure that you have the AWS CLI installed and configured. For more information, see the AWS Command Line Interface documentation.

2. Run the following `Create-Stream` command in the AWS CLI:

```
1 $ aws kinesisvideo create-stream --stream-name "MyKinesisVideoStream" --data-retention-in-
      hours "24"
```

Next Step

What's Next?

What's Next?

After you have a video stream, you can start sending data to it from a Java application. In your code, use Kinesis Video Streams options to configure your application to extract data from your media sources and upload to your stream. For more information, see Using the Java Producer Library.

Kinesis Video Streams Producer Libraries

The Amazon Kinesis Video Streams Producer libraries are a set of easy-to-use libraries that are part of the Kinesis Video Streams Producer SDK. The client uses the libraries and SDK to build the on-device application for securely connecting to Kinesis Video Streams and streaming video and other media data that can be viewed in the console or client applications in real time.

Data can be streamed media in the following ways:

- Streaming media data in real time
- Streaming media data after buffering it for a few seconds
- Streaming after-the-fact media uploads

After you create a Kinesis Video Streams stream, you can start sending data to the stream. You can use the SDK to create application code that extracts the video data (frames) from the media source and uploads it to Kinesis Video Streams. These applications are also referred to as *producer* applications.

The Producer libraries contain the following components:

- Kinesis Video Streams Producer Client
- Kinesis Video Streams Producer Library

Kinesis Video Streams Producer Client

The Kinesis Video Streams Producer Client includes a single `KinesisVideoClient` class. This class manages media sources, receives data from the sources, and manages the stream lifecycle as data flows from a media source to Kinesis Video Streams. Furthermore, it provides a `MediaSource` interface for defining the interaction between Kinesis Video Streams and your proprietary hardware and software.

A media source can be almost anything. For example, you can use a camera media source or a microphone media source. Media sources are not limited to audio and video sources only. For example, data logs might be text files, but they can still be sent as a stream of data. You could also have multiple cameras on your phone that stream data simultaneously.

To get data from any of these sources, you can implement the `MediaSource` interface. This interface enables additional scenarios for which we don't provide built-in support. For example, you might choose to send the following to Kinesis Video Streams:

- A diagnostic data stream (for example, application logs and events)
- Data from infrared cameras, RADARs, or depth cameras

Kinesis Video Streams does not provide built-in implementations for media-producing devices such as cameras. To extract data from these devices, you must implement code, thus creating your own custom media source implementation. You can then explicitly register your custom media sources with `KinesisVideoClient`, which uploads the data to Kinesis Video Streams.

The Kinesis Video Streams Producer Client is available for Java and Android applications. For more information, see Using the Java Producer Library and Using the Android Producer Library.

Kinesis Video Streams Producer Library

The Kinesis Video Streams Producer Library is contained within the Kinesis Video Streams Producer Client. The library is also available to use directly for those who want a deeper integration with Kinesis Video Streams. It enables integration from devices with proprietary operating systems, network stacks, or limited on-device resources.

The Kinesis Video Streams Producer Library implements the state machine for streaming to Kinesis Video Streams. It provides callback hooks, which require that you provide your own transport implementation and explicitly handle each message going to and from the service.

You might choose to use the Kinesis Video Streams Producer Library directly for the following reasons:

- The device on which you want to run the application doesn't have a Java virtual machine.
- You want to write application code in languages other than Java.
- You might have Java on the device, but you want to reduce the amount of overhead in your code and limit it to the bare minimum level of abstraction, due to limitations such as memory and processing power.

Currently, the Kinesis Video Streams Producer Library is available for C++ applications. For more information, see Using the C++ Producer Library.

Related Topics

Using the Java Producer Library

Using the Android Producer Library

Using the C++ Producer Library

Using the Java Producer Library

Amazon Kinesis Video Streams provides the Java Producer Library, which you can use to write application code, with minimal configuration, to send media data from a device to a Kinesis video stream.

You must perform the following steps to integrate your code with Kinesis Video Streams, so that your application can start streaming data to your Kinesis video stream:

1. Create an instance of the `KinesisVideoClient` object.

2. Create a `MediaSource` object by providing media source information. For example, when creating a camera media source, you provide information such as identifying the camera and specifying the encoding the camera uses.

   When you want to start streaming, you must create a custom media source.

3. Register the media source with `KinesisVideoClient`.

   After you register the media source with `KinesisVideoClient`, whenever the data becomes available with the media source, it calls `KinesisVideoClient` with the data.

Procedure: Using the Java Producer SDK

This procedure demonstrates how to use the Kinesis Video Streams Java Producer Client in your Java application to send data to your Kinesis video stream.

These steps don't require you to have a media source, such as a camera or microphone. Instead, for testing purposes, the code generates sample frames that consist of a series of bytes. You can use the same coding pattern when you send media data from real sources such as cameras and microphones.

The procedure includes the following steps:

- Download and Configure the Code
- Write and Examine the Code
- Run and Verify the Code

Prerequisites

- In the sample code, you provide credentials by specifying a profile that you set up in your AWS credentials profile file. If you haven't already done so, first set up your credentials profile. For more information, see Set up AWS Credentials and Region for Development in the *AWS SDK for Java*. **Note**
  The Java example uses a `SystemPropertiesCredentialsProvider` object to obtain your AWS credentials. The provider retrieves these credentials from the `aws.accessKeyId` and `aws.secretKey` Java system properties. You set these system properties in your Java development environment. For information about how to set Java system properties, see the documentation for your particular integrated development environment (IDE).
- Your `NativeLibraryPath` must contain your `KinesisVideoProducerJNI` file, available at https://github. com/awslabs/amazon-kinesis-video-streams-producer-sdk-cpp. The file name extension for this file depends on your operating system:
  - **KinesisVideoProducerJNI.so** for Linux
  - **KinesisVideoProducerJNI.dylib** for macOS
  - **KinesisVideoProducerJNI.dll** for Windows (not currently available) **Note**
    Pre-built libraries for macOS, Ubuntu, and Raspbian are available in **src/main/resources/lib**. For other environments, compile the C++ Producer Library.

Step 1: Download and Configure the Java Producer Library Code

In this section of the Java Producer Library procedure, you download the Java example code, import the project into your Java IDE, and configure the library locations.

For prerequisites and other details about this example, see Using the Java Producer Library.

1. Create a directory, and then clone the example source code from the GitHub repository.

```
1 $ git clone https://github.com/awslabs/amazon-kinesis-video-streams-producer-sdk-java
```

2. Open the Java integrated development environment (IDE) that you use (for example, Eclipse or JetBrains IntelliJ IDEA), and import the Apache Maven project that you downloaded:

   - **In IntelliJ IDEA: ** Choose **Import**. Navigate to the pom.xml file in the root of the downloaded package.
   - **In Eclipse:** Choose **File**, **Import**, **Maven**, **Existing Maven Projects**. Then navigate to the kinesis-video-java-demo directory.

   For more information, see the documentation for your IDE.

3. The Java example code uses the current AWS credentials. To use a different credentials profile, locate the following code in DemoAppMain.java:

```
1 final KinesisVideoClient kinesisVideoClient = KinesisVideoJavaClientFactory
2    .createKinesisVideoClient(
3        Regions.US_WEST_2,
4        AuthHelper.getSystemPropertiesCredentialsProvider());
```

   Change the code to the following:

```
1 final KinesisVideoClient kinesisVideoClient = KinesisVideoJavaClientFactory
2    .createKinesisVideoClient(
3        Regions.US_WEST_2,
4        new ProfileCredentialsProvider("credentials-profile-name"););
```

   For more information, see ProfileCredentialsProvider in the *AWS SDK for Java* reference.

Next Step

Step 2: Write and Examine the Code

Step 2: Write and Examine the Code

In this section, you examine the Java library and test code, and learn how to use the tools from the library in your own code.

The Kinesis Video Stream Parser Library contains the following tools:

- StreamingMkvReader
- FragmentMetadataVisitor
- OutputSegmentMerger
- KinesisVideoExample

StreamingMkvReader

This class reads specified MKV elements from a stream in a non-blocking way.

The following code example (from `FragmentMetadataVisitorTest`) shows how to create and use a `StreamingMkvReader` to retrieve `MkvElement` objects from an input stream called `inputStream`:

```
1  StreamingMkvReader mkvStreamReader =
2              StreamingMkvReader.createDefault(new InputStreamParserByteSource(inputStream));
3      while (mkvStreamReader.mightHaveNext()) {
4          Optional<MkvElement> mkvElement = mkvStreamReader.nextIfAvailable();
5          if (mkvElement.isPresent()) {
6              mkvElement.get().accept(fragmentVisitor);
7              ...
8          }
9      }
10     }
```

FragmentMetadataVisitor

This class retrieves metadata for fragments (media elements) and tracks (individual data streams containing media information, such as codec private data, pixel width, or pixel height).

The following code example (from the `FragmentMetadataVisitorTest` file) shows how to use `FragmentMetadataVisitor` to retrieve data from a `MkvElement` object:

```
1  FragmentMetadataVisitor fragmentVisitor = FragmentMetadataVisitor.create();
2      StreamingMkvReader mkvStreamReader =
3              StreamingMkvReader.createDefault(new InputStreamParserByteSource(in));
4      int segmentCount = 0;
5      while(mkvStreamReader.mightHaveNext()) {
6          Optional<MkvElement> mkvElement = mkvStreamReader.nextIfAvailable();
7          if (mkvElement.isPresent()) {
8              mkvElement.get().accept(fragmentVisitor);
9              if (MkvTypeInfos.SIMPLEBLOCK.equals(mkvElement.get().getElementMetaData().
                   getTypeInfo())) {
10                 MkvDataElement dataElement = (MkvDataElement) mkvElement.get();
11                 Frame frame = ((MkvValue<Frame>)dataElement.getValueCopy()).getVal();
12                 MkvTrackMetadata trackMetadata = fragmentVisitor.getMkvTrackMetadata(frame.
                       getTrackNumber());
13                 assertTrackAndFragmentInfo(fragmentVisitor, frame, trackMetadata);
14             }
```

```
15              if (MkvTypeInfos.SEGMENT.equals(mkvElement.get().getElementMetaData().
                    getTypeInfo())) {
16                  if (mkvElement.get() instanceof MkvEndMasterElement) {
17                      if (segmentCount < continuationTokens.size()) {
18                          Optional<String> continuationToken = fragmentVisitor.
                                getContinuationToken();
19                          Assert.assertTrue(continuationToken.isPresent());
20                          Assert.assertEquals(continuationTokens.get(segmentCount),
                                continuationToken.get());
21                      }
22                      segmentCount++;
23                  }
24              }
25          }
26
27      }
```

The preceding example shows the following coding pattern:

- Create a `FragmentMetadataVisitor` to parse the data, and a StreamingMkvReader to provide the data.
- For each `MkvElement` in the stream, test if its metadata is of type `SIMPLEBLOCK`.
- If it is, retrieve the `MkvDataElement` from the `MkvElement`.
- Retrieve the `Frame` (media data) from the `MkvDataElement`.
- Retrieve the `MkvTrackMetadata` for the `Frame` from the `FragmentMetadataVisitor`.
- Retrieve and verify the following data from the `Frame` and `MkvTrackMetadata` objects:
  - The track number.
  - The frame's pixel height.
  - The frame's pixel width.
  - The codec ID for the codec used to encode the frame.
  - That this frame arrived in order. That is, verify that the track number of the previous frame, if present, is less than that of the current frame.

To use `FragmentMetadataVisitor` in your project, pass `MkvElement` objects to the visitor using their `accept` method:

```
1 mkvElement.get().accept(fragmentVisitor);
```

OutputSegmentMerger

This class merges metadata from different tracks in the stream into a stream with a single segment.

The following code example (from the `FragmentMetadataVisitorTest` file) shows how to use `OutputSegmentMerger` to merge track metadata from a byte array called `inputBytes`:

```
1 FragmentMetadataVisitor fragmentVisitor = FragmentMetadataVisitor.create();
2
3 ByteArrayOutputStream outputStream = new ByteArrayOutputStream();
4
5 OutputSegmentMerger outputSegmentMerger =
6     OutputSegmentMerger.createDefault(outputStream);
7
8 CompositeMkvElementVisitor compositeVisitor =
9     new TestCompositeVisitor(fragmentVisitor, outputSegmentMerger);
10
11 final InputStream in = TestResourceUtil.getTestInputStream("output_get_media.mkv");
12
```

```
13 StreamingMkvReader mkvStreamReader =
14     StreamingMkvReader.createDefault(new InputStreamParserByteSource(in));
15
16 while (mkvStreamReader.mightHaveNext()) {
17     Optional<MkvElement> mkvElement = mkvStreamReader.nextIfAvailable();
18     if (mkvElement.isPresent()) {
19         mkvElement.get().accept(compositeVisitor);
20     if (MkvTypeInfos.SIMPLEBLOCK.equals(mkvElement.get().getElementMetaData().getTypeInfo())) {
21         MkvDataElement dataElement = (MkvDataElement) mkvElement.get();
22         Frame frame = ((MkvValue<Frame>) dataElement.getValueCopy()).getVal();
23         Assert.assertTrue(frame.getFrameData().limit() > 0);
24         MkvTrackMetadata trackMetadata = fragmentVisitor.getMkvTrackMetadata(frame.
                getTrackNumber());
25         assertTrackAndFragmentInfo(fragmentVisitor, frame, trackMetadata);
26     }
27 }
```

The preceding example shows the following coding pattern:

- Create a FragmentMetadataVisitorto retrieve the metadata from the stream.
- Create an output stream to receive the merged metadata.
- Create an `OutputSegmentMerger`, passing in the `ByteArrayOutputStream`.
- Create a `CompositeMkvElementVisitor` that contains the two visitors.
- Create an `InputStream` that points to the specified file.
- Merge each element in the input data into the output stream.

KinesisVideoExample

This is a sample application that shows how to use the Kinesis Video Stream Parser Library.

This class performs the following operations:

- Creates a Kinesis video stream. If a stream with the given name already exists, the stream is deleted and recreated.
- Calls PutMedia to stream video fragments to the Kinesis video stream.
- Calls GetMedia to stream video fragments out of the Kinesis video stream.
- Uses a StreamingMkvReader to parse the returned fragments on the stream, and uses a FragmentMetadataVisitor to log the fragments.

Delete and recreate the stream

The following code example (from the `StreamOps.java` file) deletes a given Kinesis video stream:

```
1 //Delete the stream
2 amazonKinesisVideo.deleteStream(new DeleteStreamRequest().withStreamARN(streamInfo.get().
    getStreamARN()));
```

The following code example (from the `StreamOps.java` file) creates a Kinesis video stream with the specified name:

```
1 amazonKinesisVideo.createStream(new CreateStreamRequest().withStreamName(streamName)
2 .withDataRetentionInHours(DATA_RETENTION_IN_HOURS)
3 .withMediaType("video/h264"));
```

Call PutMedia

The following code example (from the `PutMediaWorker.java` file) calls PutMedia on the stream:

```
1 putMedia.putMedia(new PutMediaRequest().withStreamName(streamName)
2 .withFragmentTimecodeType(FragmentTimecodeType.RELATIVE)
3 .withProducerStartTimestamp(new Date())
4 .withPayload(inputStream), new PutMediaAckResponseHandler() {
5 ...
6 });
```

Call GetMedia

The following code example (from the `GetMediaWorker.java` file) calls GetMedia on the stream:

```
1 GetMediaResult result = videoMedia.getMedia(new GetMediaRequest().withStreamName(streamName).
      withStartSelector(startSelector));
```

Parse the GetMedia result

This section describes how to use StreamingMkvReader, FragmentMetadataVisitor and `CompositeMkvElementVisitor` to parse, save to file, and log the data returned from `GetMedia`.

Read the output of GetMedia with StreamingMkvReader

The following code example (from the `GetMediaWorker.java` file) creates a StreamingMkvReader and uses it to parse the result from the GetMedia operation:

```
1 StreamingMkvReader mkvStreamReader = StreamingMkvReader.createDefault(new
      InputStreamParserByteSource(result.getPayload()));
2 log.info("StreamingMkvReader created for stream {} ", streamName);
3 try {
4     mkvStreamReader.apply(this.elementVisitor);
5 } catch (MkvElementVisitException e) {
6     log.error("Exception while accepting visitor {}", e);
7 }
```

In the preceding code example, the StreamingMkvReader retrieves `MKVElement` objects from the payload of the `GetMedia` result. In the next section, the elements are passed to a FragmentMetadataVisitor.

Retrieve Fragments with FragmentMetadataVisitor

The following code examples (from the `KinesisVideoExample.java` and `StreamingMkvReader.java` files) create a FragmentMetadataVisitor. The `MkvElement` objects iterated by the StreamingMkvReader are then passed to the visitor using the `accept` method.

from KinesisVideoExample.java:

```
1 FragmentMetadataVisitor fragmentMetadataVisitor = FragmentMetadataVisitor.create();
```

from StreamingMkvReader.java:

```
1 if (mkvElementOptional.isPresent()) {
2     //Apply the MkvElement to the visitor
3     mkvElementOptional.get().accept(elementVisitor);
4         }
```

Log the elements and write them to a file

The following code example (from the `KinesisVideoExample.java` file) creates the following objects and returns them as part of the return value of the `GetMediaProcessingArguments` function:

- A `LogVisitor` (an extension of `MkvElementVisitor`) that writes to the system log.
- An `OutputStream` that writes the incoming data to an MKV file.
- A `BufferedOutputStream` that buffers data bound for the `OutputStream`.
- An OutputSegmentMerger that merges consecutive elements in the `GetMedia` result with the same track and EBML data.
- A `CompositeMkvElementVisitor` that composes the FragmentMetadataVisitor, OutputSegmentMerger, and LogVisitor into a single element visitor

```
1   //A visitor used to log as the GetMedia stream is processed.
2       LogVisitor logVisitor = new LogVisitor(fragmentMetadataVisitor);
3
4       //An OutputSegmentMerger to combine multiple segments that share track and ebml metadata
            into one
5       //mkv segment.
6       OutputStream fileOutputStream = Files.newOutputStream(Paths.get("
            kinesis_video_example_merged_output2.mkv"),
7           StandardOpenOption.WRITE, StandardOpenOption.CREATE);
8       BufferedOutputStream outputStream = new BufferedOutputStream(fileOutputStream);
9       OutputSegmentMerger outputSegmentMerger = OutputSegmentMerger.createDefault(outputStream);
10
11      //A composite visitor to encapsulate the three visitors.
12      CompositeMkvElementVisitor mkvElementVisitor =
13          new CompositeMkvElementVisitor(fragmentMetadataVisitor, outputSegmentMerger,
                logVisitor);
14
15      return new GetMediaProcessingArguments(outputStream, logVisitor, mkvElementVisitor);
```

The media processing arguments are then passed into the `GetMediaWorker`, which is in turn passed to the `ExecutorService` which executes the worker on a separate thread:

```
1   GetMediaWorker getMediaWorker = GetMediaWorker.create(getRegion(),
2       getCredentialsProvider(),
3       getStreamName(),
4       new StartSelector().withStartSelectorType(StartSelectorType.EARLIEST),
5       amazonKinesisVideo,
6       getMediaProcessingArgumentsLocal.getMkvElementVisitor());
7   executorService.submit(getMediaWorker);
```

Next Step

Step 3: Run and Verify the Code

Step 3: Run and Verify the Code

The Kinesis Video Stream Parser Library contains tools that are intended for you to use in your own projects. The project contains unit tests for the tools that you can run to verify your installation.

The following unit tests are included in the library:

- **mkv**
  - ElementSizeAndOffsetVisitorTest
  - MkvValueTest
  - StreamingMkvReaderTest
- **utilities**
  - FragmentMetadataVisitorTest
  - OutputSegmentMergerTest

Using the Android Producer Library

Amazon Kinesis Video Streams provides the Android Producer Library, which you can use to write application code, with minimal configuration, to send media data from an Android device to a Kinesis video stream.

You must perform the following steps to integrate your code with Kinesis Video Streams so that your application can start streaming data to your Kinesis video stream:

1. Create an instance of the `KinesisVideoClient` object.

2. Create a `MediaSource` object by providing media source information. For example, when creating a camera media source, you provide information such as identifying the camera and specifying the encoding the camera uses.

   When you want to start streaming, you must create a custom media source.

Procedure: Using the Android Producer SDK

This procedure demonstrates how to use the Kinesis Video Streams Android Producer Client in your Android application to send data to your Kinesis video stream.

The procedure includes the following steps:

- Download and Configure the Code
- Examine the Code
- Run and Verify the Code

Prerequisites

- We recommend Android Studio for examining, editing, and running the application code. We recommend at least version 3.0.0, released October 2017.
- In the sample code, you provide Amazon Cognito credentials. Follow these procedures to set up an Amazon Cognito user pool and identity pool:

To set up a user pool

1. Sign in to the Amazon Cognito console.

2. Choose **Manage your User Pools**.

3. Choose **Create a user pool**.

4. Type a value for **Pool name**; for example, _android_user_pool.

5. Choose **Review defaults**.

6. Choose **Create pool**.

7. Copy and save the **Pool Id** value. You will need this value when you configure the example application.

8. On the page for your pool, choose **App clients**.

9. Choose **Add an app client**.

10. Type a value for **App client name**; for example, _android_app_client.

11. Choose **Create app client**.

12. Choose **Show Details**, and copy and save the **App client ID** and **App client secret**. You will need these values when you configure the example application.

To set up an identity pool

1. Open the Amazon Cognito console.

2. Choose **Manage Federated Identities**.

3. Choose **Create new identity pool**.

4. Type a value for **Identity pool name**; for example, _android_identity_pool.

5. Expand the **Authentication providers** section. On the **Cognito** tab, add the values for the **User Pool ID** and **App client ID** from the previous procedure.

6. Choose **Create pool**.

7. On the next page, expand the **Show Details** section.

8. In the section that has a value for **Role name** that ends in **Auth_Role**, choose **View Policy Document**.

9. Choose **Edit**, and confirm the **Edit Policy** dialog box that appears. Then copy the following JSON and paste it into the editor:

```
1  {
2      "Version": "2012-10-17",
3      "Statement": [
4      {
5        "Effect": "Allow",
6        "Action": [
7          "cognito-identity:*",
8          "kinesisvideo:*"
9        ],
10       "Resource": [
11         "*"
12       ]
13     }
14   ]
15 }
```

10. Choose **Allow**.

11. On the next page, copy and save the **Identity pool ID** value from the **Get AWS Credentials** code snippet. You will need this value when you configure the example application.

Step 1: Download and Configure the Android Producer Library Code

In this section of the Android Producer Library procedure, you download the Android example code and open the project in Android Studio.

For prerequisites and other details about this example, see Using the Android Producer Library.

1. Create a directory, and then clone the AWS Android SDK from the GitHub repository.

```
1  $ git clone https://github.com/awslabs/aws-sdk-android-samples
```

2. Open Android Studio.

3. In the opening screen, choose **Open an existing Android Studio project**.

4. Navigate to the `aws-sdk-android-samples/AmazonKinesisVideoDemoApp` directory, and choose **OK**.

5. Open the `AmazonKinesisVideoDemoApp/src/main/res/raw/awsconfiguration.json` file.

   In the `CredentialsProvider` node, provide the identity pool ID from the **To set up an identity pool** procedure in the Prerequisites section, and provide your AWS Region (for example, **us-west-2**).

   In the `CognitoUserPool` node, provide the App client secret, App client ID, and Pool ID from the **To set up a user pool** procedure in the Prerequisites section, and provide your AWS Region (for example, **us-west-2**).

6. Your `awsconfiguration.json` file will look similar to the following:

```
1  {
2    "Version": "1.0",
3    "CredentialsProvider": {
4      "CognitoIdentity": {
5        "Default": {
6          "PoolId": "us-west-2:01234567-89ab-cdef-0123-456789abcdef",
7          "Region": "us-west-2"
8        }
9      }
10   },
11   "IdentityManager": {
12     "Default": {}
13   },
14   "CognitoUserPool": {
15     "Default": {
16       "AppClientSecret": "abcdefghijklmnopqrstuvwxyz0123456789abcdefghijklmno",
17       "AppClientId": "0123456789abcdefghijklmnop",
18       "PoolId": "us-west-2_qRsTuVwXy",
19       "Region": "us-west-2"
20     }
21   }
22 }
```

7. Update the `StreamingFragment.java` file with your region:

```
1  try {
2    mKinesisVideoClient = KinesisVideoAndroidClientFactory.createKinesisVideoClient(
3    getActivity(),
4    Regions.US_WEST_2,
5    KinesisVideoDemoApp.getCredentialsProvider());
```

   For AWS region constants, see Regions.

Next Step

Step 2: Examine the Code

Step 2: Examine the Code

In this section of the Android Producer Library procedure, you examine the example code.

The Android test application (`AmazonKinesisVideoDemoApp`) shows the following coding pattern:

- Create an instance of `KinesisVideoClient`.
- Create an instance of `MediaSource`.
- Start streaming—that is, start the `MediaSource`, and it starts sending data to the client.

The following sections provide details.

Creating an Instance of KinesisVideoClient

You create the `KinesisVideoClient` object by calling the `createKinesisVideoClient` operation.

```
1 mKinesisVideoClient = KinesisVideoAndroidClientFactory.createKinesisVideoClient(
2                 getActivity(),
3                 Regions.US_WEST_2,
4                 KinesisVideoDemoApp.getCredentialsProvider());
```

For `KinesisVideoClient` to make network calls, it needs credentials to authenticate. You pass in an instance of `AWSCredentialsProvider`, which reads your Amazon Cognito credentials from the `awsconfiguration.json` file that you modified in the previous section.

Creating an Instance of MediaSource

To send bytes to your Kinesis video stream, you must produce the data. Amazon Kinesis Video Streams provides the `MediaSource` interface, which represents the data source.

For example, the Kinesis Video Streams Android library provides the `AndroidCameraMediaSource` implementation of the `MediaSource` interface. This class reads data from one of the device's cameras.

In the following code example (from the `fragment/StreamConfigurationFragment.java` file), the configuration for the media source is created:

```
1 private AndroidCameraMediaSourceConfiguration getCurrentConfiguration() {
2 return new AndroidCameraMediaSourceConfiguration(
3       AndroidCameraMediaSourceConfiguration.builder()
4             .withCameraId(mCamerasDropdown.getSelectedItem().getCameraId())
5             .withEncodingMimeType(mMimeTypeDropdown.getSelectedItem().getMimeType())
6             .withHorizontalResolution(mResolutionDropdown.getSelectedItem().getWidth())
7             .withVerticalResolution(mResolutionDropdown.getSelectedItem().getHeight())
8             .withCameraFacing(mCamerasDropdown.getSelectedItem().getCameraFacing())
9             .withIsEncoderHardwareAccelerated(
10                   mCamerasDropdown.getSelectedItem().isEndcoderHardwareAccelerated())
11            .withFrameRate(FRAMERATE_20)
12            .withRetentionPeriodInHours(RETENTION_PERIOD_48_HOURS)
13            .withEncodingBitRate(BITRATE_384_KBPS)
14            .withCameraOrientation(-mCamerasDropdown.getSelectedItem().getCameraOrientation
                  ())
15            .withNalAdaptationFlags(StreamInfo.NalAdaptationFlags.
                  NAL_ADAPTATION_ANNEXB_CPD_AND_FRAME_NALS)
16            .withIsAbsoluteTimecode(false));
17 }
```

In the following code example (from the `fragment/StreamingFragment.java` file), the media source is created:

```
1 mCameraMediaSource = (AndroidCameraMediaSource) mKinesisVideoClient
2     .createMediaSource(mStreamName, mConfiguration);
```

Starting the Media Source

Start the media source so that it can begin generating data and sending it to the client. The following code example is from the `fragment/StreamingFragment.java` file:

```
1 mCameraMediaSource.start();
```

Next Step

Step 3: Run and Verify the Code

Using the C++ Producer Library

Amazon Kinesis Video Streams provides the C++ Producer Library, which you can use to write application code to send media data from a device to a Kinesis video stream.

Object Model

The C++ library provides the following objects to manage sending data to a Kinesis video stream:

- **KinesisVideoProducer:** Contains information about your media source and AWS credentials, and maintains callbacks to report on Kinesis Video Streams events.
- **KinesisVideoStream:** Represents the Kinesis video stream. Contains information about the video stream's parameters, such as name, data retention period, media content type, and so on.

Putting Media into the Stream

The C++ library provides methods (for example, `PutFrame`) that you can use to put data into the `KinesisVideoStream` object. The library then manages the internal state of the data, which can include the following tasks:

- Performing authentication.
- Watching for network latency. If the latency is too high, the library might choose to drop frames.
- Tracking status of streaming in progress.

Callback Interfaces

This layer exposes a set of callback interfaces, which enable it to talk to the application layer. These callback interfaces include the following:

- Service callbacks interface (`CallbackProvider`): The library invokes events obtained through this interface when it creates a stream, obtains a stream description, deletes a stream, and so on.
- Client-ready state or low storage events interface (`ClientCallbackProvider`): The library invokes events on this interface when the client is ready, or when it detects that it might run out of available storage or memory.
- Stream events callback interface (`StreamCallbackProvider`): The library invokes events on this interface when stream events occur, such as the stream entering the ready state, dropped frames, or stream errors.

Kinesis Video Streams provides default implementations for these interfaces. You can also provide your own custom implementation—for example, if you need custom networking logic or you want to expose a low storage condition to the user interface.

For more information on callbacks in the Producer Libraries, see Producer SDK Callbacks.

Procedure: Using the C++ Producer SDK

This procedure demonstrates how to use the Kinesis Video Streams client and media sources in a C++ application to send data to your Kinesis video stream.

Note
The C++ library includes a sample build script for macOS. The C++ Producer Library is not currently available for Windows.
To use the C++ Producer Library on a Raspberry Pi device, see Appendix: Using the C++ Producer SDK on Raspberry Pi.

The procedure includes the following steps:

- Step 1: Download and Configure the Code
- Step 2: Write and Examine the Code
- Step 3: Run and Verify the Code

Prerequisites

- **Credentials:** In the sample code, you provide credentials by specifying a profile that you set up in your AWS credentials profile file. If you haven't already done so, first set up your credentials profile.

  For more information, see Set up AWS Credentials and Region for Development.

- **Certificate store integration:** The Kinesis Video Streams Producer Library must establish trust with the service it calls. This is done through validating the certification authorities (CAs) in the public certificate store. On Linux-based models, this store is located in the `/etc/ssl/` directory.

  Download the certificate from the following location to your certificate store:

  https://www.amazontrust.com/repository/SFSRootCAG2.pem

- Install the following build dependencies for macOS:
  - Autoconf 2.69 (License GPLv3+/Autoconf: GNU GPL version 3 or later)
  - CMake 3.7 or 3.8
  - Pkg-Config
  - Flex 2.5.35 Apple (flex-31) or later
  - Bison 2.4 (GNU License)
  - Automake 1.15.1 (GNU License)
  - GNU Libtool (Apple Inc. version cctools-898)
  - xCode (macOS) / clang / gcc (xcode-select version 2347)
  - Java Development Kit (JDK) (for Java JNI compilation)
  - Lib-Pkg

- Install the following build dependencies for Ubuntu (responses to version commands are truncated):
  - Install Git: `sudo apt-get install git`

    ```
    1 $ git --version
    2 git version 2.14.1
    ```

  - Install CMake: `sudo apt-get install cmake`

    ```
    1 $ cmake --version
    2 cmake version 3.9.1
    ```

  - Install Libtool: `sudo apt-get install libtool`

    ```
    1 2.4.6-2
    ```

  - Install libtool-bin: `sudo apt-get install libtool-bin`

    ```
    1 $ libtool --version
    2 libtool (GNU libtool) 2.4.6
    3 Written by Gordon Matzigkeit, 1996
    ```

  - Install GNU Automake: `sudo apt-get install automake`

    ```
    1 $ automake --version
    2 automake (GNU automake) 1.15
    ```

- Install GNU Bison: `sudo apt-get install bison`

```
1 $ bison -V
2 bison (GNU Bison) 3.0.4
```

- Install G++: `sudo apt-get install g++`

```
1 g++ --version
2 g++ (Ubuntu 7.2.0-8ubuntu3) 7.2.0
```

- Install curl: `sudo apt-get install curl`

```
1 $ curl --version
2 curl 7.55.1 (x86_64-pc-linux-gnu) libcurl/7.55.1 OpenSSL/1.0.2g zlib/1.2.11 libidn2
      /2.0.2 libpsl/0.18.0 (+libidn2/2.0.2) librtmp/2.3
```

- Install pkg-config: `sudo apt-get install pkg-config`

```
1 $ pkg-config --version
2 0.29.1
```

- Install Flex: `sudo apt-get install flex`

```
1 $ flex --version
2 flex 2.6.1
```

- Install OpenJDK: `sudo apt-get install openjdk-8-jdk`

```
1 $ java -showversion
2 openjdk version "1.8.0_151"
```

- Set the `JAVA_HOME` environment variable: `export JAVA_HOME=/usr/lib/jvm/java-8-openjdk-amd64/`

- Run the build script: `./install-script`

Next Step

Step 1: Download and Configure the C++ Producer Library Code

Step 1: Download and Configure the C++ Producer Library Code

In this section, you download the low-level libraries and configure the application to use your AWS credentials. For prerequisites and other details about this example, see Using the C++ Producer Library.

1. Create a directory, and then clone the example source code from the GitHub repository.

```
1  $ git clone https://github.com/awslabs/amazon-kinesis-video-streams-producer-sdk-cpp
```

2. Open the code in the integrated development environment (IDE) of your choice (for example, Eclipse).

3. At the command line, set the `ACCESS_KEY_ENV_VAR` and `SECRET_KEY_ENV_VAR` environment variables to your AWS credentials. Alternatively, you can hardcode your AWS credentials in the following lines of `ProducerTestFixture.h`:

```
1          if (nullptr == (accessKey = getenv(ACCESS_KEY_ENV_VAR))) {
2              accessKey = "AccessKey";
3          }
4
5          if (nullptr == (secretKey = getenv(SECRET_KEY_ENV_VAR))) {
6              secretKey = "SecretKey";
7          }
```

4. In `tst/ProducerTestFixture.h`, find the call to `CreateStream`. Change the name of the stream definition from ScaryTestStream2 to a unique name:

```
1  shared_ptr<KinesisVideoStream> CreateTestStream(int index) {
2          char stream_name[MAX_STREAM_NAME_LEN];
3          sprintf(stream_name, "ScaryTestStream_%d", index);
```

Next Step

Step 2: Write and Examine the Code

Using the C++ Producer SDK as a GStreamer Plugin

GStreamer is a popular media framework used by a multitude of cameras and video sources to create custom media pipelines by combining modular plugins. The Kinesis Video Streams GStreamer plugin greatly simplifies the integration of your existing GStreamer media pipeline with Kinesis Video Streams.

For information on using the C++ Producer SDK as a GStreamer plugin, see Example: Kinesis Video Streams Producer SDK GStreamer Plugin.

Using the C++ Producer SDK as a GStreamer Plugin in a Docker Container

GStreamer is a popular media framework used by a multitude of cameras and video sources to create custom media pipelines by combining modular plugins. The Kinesis Video Streams GStreamer plugin greatly simplifies the integration of your existing GStreamer media pipeline with Kinesis Video Streams.

In addition, using Docker to create the GStreamer pipeline standardizes the operating environment for Kinesis Video Streams, which greatly simplifies building and executing the application.

For information on using the C++ Producer SDK as a GStreamer plugin in a Docker container, see Run the GStreamer Element in a Docker Container.

Appendix: Using the C++ Producer SDK on Raspberry Pi

The Raspberry Pi is a small, inexpensive computer that can be used to teach and learn basic computer programming skills. This tutorial describes how you can set up and use the Amazon Kinesis Video Streams C++ Producer SDK on a Raspberry Pi device. The steps also include how to verify the installation using the GStreamer demo application.

Topics

- Prerequisites
- Create an IAM User with Permission to Write to Kinesis Video Streams
- Join Your Raspberry Pi to Your Wi-Fi Network
- Connect Remotely to Your Raspberry Pi
- Configure the Raspberry Pi Camera
- Install Software Prerequisites
- Download and Build the Kinesis Video Streams C++ Producer SDK
- Stream Video to Your Kinesis Video Stream and View the Live Stream

Prerequisites

Before you set up the C++ Producer SDK on your Raspberry Pi, ensure that you have the following prerequisites:

- A Raspberry Pi device with the following configuration:
  - Board version: 3 Model B or later.
  - A connected camera module.
  - An SD card with a capacity of at least 8 GB.
  - The Raspbian operating system (kernel version 4.9 or later) installed. You can download the latest Raspbian image from the Raspberry Pi Foundation website. Follow the Raspberry Pi instructions to install the downloaded image on an SD card.
- An AWS account with a Kinesis video stream. For more information, see Getting Started with Kinesis Video Streams.

Create an IAM User with Permission to Write to Kinesis Video Streams

If you haven't already done so, set up an AWS Identity and Access Management (IAM) user with permissions to write to a Kinesis video stream.

1. Sign in to the AWS Management Console and open the IAM console at https://console.aws.amazon.com/iam/.
2. In the navigation menu on the left, choose **Users**.
3. To create a new user, choose **Add user**.
4. Provide a descriptive **User name** for the user, such as **kinesis-video-raspberry-pi-producer**.
5. Under **Access type**, choose **Programmatic access**.
6. Choose **Next: Permissions**.
7. Under **Set permissions for kinesis-video-raspberry-pi-producer**, choose **Attach existing policies directly**.
8. Choose **Create policy**. The **Create policy** page opens in a new web browser tab.
9. Choose the **JSON** tab.
10. Copy the following JSON policy and paste it into the text area. This policy gives your user permission to create and write data to Kinesis video streams.

```
1  {
2    "Version": "2012-10-17",
3    "Statement": [{
4      "Effect": "Allow",
5        "Action": [
6        "kinesisvideo:DescribeStream",
7        "kinesisvideo:CreateStream",
8        "kinesisvideo:GetDataEndpoint",
9        "kinesisvideo:PutMedia"
10      ],
11      "Resource": [
12        "*"
13      ]
14    }]
15  }
```

11. Choose **Review policy**.

12. Provide a **Name** for your policy, such as **kinesis-video-stream-write-policy**.

13. Choose **Create policy**.

14. Return to the **Add user** tab in your browser, and choose **Refresh**.

15. In the search box, type the name of the policy you created.

16. Select the check box next to your new policy in the list.

17. Choose **Next: Review**.

18. Choose **Create user**.

19. The console displays the **Access key ID** for your new user. Choose **Show** to display the **Secret access key**. Record these values; they are required when you configure the application.

Join Your Raspberry Pi to Your Wi-Fi Network

You can use the Raspberry Pi in *headless* mode, that is, without an attached keyboard, monitor, or network cable. If you are using an attached monitor and keyboard, proceed to Configure the Raspberry Pi Camera.

1. On your computer, create a file named `wpa_supplicant.conf`.

2. Copy the following text and paste it into the `wpa_supplicant.conf` file (or download a sample wpa_supplicant.conf file):

```
1  country=US
2  ctrl_interface=DIR=/var/run/wpa_supplicant GROUP=netdev
3  update_config=1
4
5  network={
6  ssid="<YOUR_WIFI_SSID>"
7  scan_ssid=1
8  key_mgmt=WPA-PSK
9  psk="<YOUR_WIFI_PASSWORD>"
10 }
```

Replace the `ssid` and `psk` values with the information for your Wi-Fi network.

3. Copy the `wpa_supplicant.conf` file to the SD card. It must be copied to the root of the `boot` volume.

4. Insert the SD card into the Raspberry Pi, and power the device. It joins your Wi-Fi network, and SSH is enabled.

Connect Remotely to Your Raspberry Pi

You can connect remotely to your Raspberry Pi in headless mode. If you are using your Raspberry Pi with a connected monitor and keyboard, proceed to Configure the Raspberry Pi Camera.

1. Before connecting to your Raspberry Pi device remotely, do one of the following to determine its IP address:

   - If you have access to your network's Wi-Fi router, look at the connected Wi-Fi devices. Find the device named `Raspberry Pi` to find your device's IP address.
   - If you don't have access to your network's Wi-Fi router, you can use other software to find devices on your network. Fing is a popular application that is available for both Android and iOS devices. You can use the free version of this application to find the IP addresses of devices on your network.

2. When you know the IP address of the Raspberry Pi device, you can use any terminal application to connect.

   - On macOS or Linux, use `ssh`:

   ```
   1 $ ssh pi@<IP address>
   ```

   - On Windows, use PuTTY, a free SSH client for Windows.

   For a new installation of Raspbian, the user name is **pi**, and the password is **raspberry**. We recommend that you change the default password.

Configure the Raspberry Pi Camera

Follow these steps to configure the Raspberry Pi camera to send video from the device to a Kinesis video stream.

1. Open an editor to update the `modules` file with the following command:

```
1 $ sudo nano /etc/modules
```

2. Add the following line to the end of the file, if it's not already there:

```
1 bcm2835-v4l2
```

3. Save the file and exit the editor (Ctrl-X).

4. Reboot the Raspberry Pi:

```
1 $ sudo reboot
```

5. When the device reboots, connect to it again through your terminal application if you are connecting remotely.

6. Open `raspi-config`:

```
1 $ sudo raspi-config
```

7. Choose **Interfacing Options**, **Camera**. Enable the camera if it's not already enabled, and reboot if prompted.

8. Verify that the camera is working by typing the following command:

```
1 $ raspistill -v -o test.jpg
```

The display shows a five-second preview from the camera, takes a picture (saved to `test.jpg`), and displays informational messages.

Install Software Prerequisites

The C++ Producer SDK requires that you install the following software prerequisites on Raspberry Pi.

1. Install Git:

```
1 $  sudo apt-get update
2 $  sudo apt-get install git
```

2. Install Yacc, Lex, and OpenJDK (Open Java Development Kit):

```
1 $  sudo apt-get install byacc flex
2 $  sudo apt-get install openjdk-8-jdk
```

3. Set the JAVA_HOME environment variable:

```
1 $  export JAVA_HOME=/usr/lib/jvm/java-1.8.0-openjdk-armhf/
```

Note
If you reboot the device before building the SDK, you must repeat this step. You can also set this environment variable in your ~/.profile file.

1. CMake is used to build the SDK. Install CMake with the following command:

```
1 $  sudo apt-get install cmake
```

2. Copy the following PEM file to /etc/ssl/cert.pem:

https://www.amazontrust.com/repository/SFSRootCAG2.pem

Download and Build the Kinesis Video Streams C++ Producer SDK

1. Install the C++ Producer SDK:

```
1 $  git clone https://github.com/awslabs/amazon-kinesis-video-streams-producer-sdk-cpp
```

2. Change your current working directory to the install directory:

```
1 $  cd amazon-kinesis-video-stream-producer-sdk-cpp/kinesis-video-native-build
```

3. Make the install script executable:

```
1 $  chmod +x install-script
```

4. Run the install script. The script downloads the source and builds several open-source projects. It might take several hours to run the first time it is executed:

```
1 $  ./install-script
```

5. Type **Y** to verify. Then the build script runs.

Stream Video to Your Kinesis Video Stream and View the Live Stream

1. To run the sample application, you need the following information:
   - The name of the stream you created in the Prerequisites section.
   - The account credentials (Access Key ID and secret access key) that you created in Create an IAM User with Permission to Write to Kinesis Video Streams.
2. Run the sample application using the following command:

```
1 $ export AWS_ACCESS_KEY_ID=<Access Key ID>
2 export AWS_SECRET_ACCESS_KEY=<Secret Access Key>
3 ./kinesis_video_gstreamer_sample_app Stream Name
```

3. You can specify the image size, framerate, and bitrate as follows:

```
1 $ export AWS_ACCESS_KEY_ID=<Access Key ID>
2 export AWS_SECRET_ACCESS_KEY=<Secret Access Key>
3 ./kinesis_video_gstreamer_sample_app -w <width> -h <height> -f <framerate>
4                       -b <bitrateInKBPS> Stream Name
```

4. If the sample application exits with a `library not found` error, type the following commands to verify that the project is correctly linked to its open-source dependencies:

```
1 $  rm -rf ./kinesis-video-native-build/CMakeCache.txt ./kinesis-video-native-build/
      CMakeFiles
2 $  ./kinesis-video-native-build/install-script
```

5. Open the Kinesis Video Streams console at https://console.aws.amazon.com/kinesisvideo/.

6. Choose the **Stream name** of the stream you created.

The video stream that is sent from the Raspberry Pi appears in the console.

When the stream is playing, you can experiment with the following features of the Kinesis Video Streams console:

- In the **Video preview** section, use the navigation controls to rewind or fast-forward the stream.

- In the **Stream info** section, notice the codec, resolution, and bit rate of the stream. The resolution and bitrate values are set purposefully low on the Raspberry Pi to minimize bandwidth usage for this tutorial. To view the Amazon CloudWatch metrics that are being created for your stream, choose **View stream metrics in CloudWatch**.

- Under **Data retention period**, notice that the video stream is retained for one day. You can edit this value and set it to **No data retention**, or set a value from one day to several years.

  Under server-side encryption, notice that your data is being encrypted at rest using a key maintained by the AWS Key Management Service (AWS KMS).

Producer SDK Reference

This section contains limits, error codes, and other reference information for the Kinesis Video Streams Producer Libraries.

Topics

- Producer SDK Limits
- Error Code Reference
- Network Abstraction Layer (NAL) Adaptation Flag Reference
- Producer SDK Structures
- Kinesis Video Stream Structures
- Producer SDK Callbacks

Producer SDK Limits

The following table contains the current limits for values in the Producer Libraries.

Value	Limit	Notes
Max stream count	128	The maximum number of streams that a producer object can create. This is a soft limit (you can request an increase). It ensures that the producer doesn't accidentally create streams recursively.
Max device name length	128 characters	
Max tag count	50 per stream	
Max stream name length	256 characters	
Min storage size	10 MiB = 10 * 1024 * 1024 bytes	
Max storage size	10 GiB = 10 * 1024 * 1024 * 1024 bytes	
Max root directory path length	4,096 characters	
Max auth info length	10,000 bytes	
Max URI string length	10,000 characters	
Max tag name length	128 characters	
Max tag value length	1,024 characters	
Min security token period	30 seconds	
Security token grace period	40 minutes	If the specified duration is longer, it is limited to this value.
Retention period	0 or greater than one hour	0 indicates no retention.
Min cluster duration	1 second	The value is specified in 100 ns units, which is the SDK standard.
Max cluster duration	30 seconds	The value is specified in 100 ns units, which is the SDK standard. The backend API may enforce a shorter cluster duration.
Max fragment size	50 MB	For more information, see Kinesis Video Streams Limits.
Max fragment duration	10 seconds	For more information, see Kinesis Video Streams Limits.
Max connection duration	45 minutes	The backend closes the connection after this time. The SDK rotates the token and establishes a new connection within this time.
Max ACK segment length	1,024 characters	Maximum segment length of the acknowledgement sent to the ACK parser function.
Max content type string length	128 characters	

Value	Limit	Notes
Max codec ID string length	32 characters	
Max track name string length	32 characters	
Max codec private data length	1 MiB = 1 * 1024 * 1024 bytes	
Min timecode scale value length	100 ns	The minimum timecode scale value to represent the frame time stamps in the resulting MKV cluster. The value is specified in increments of 100 ns, which is the SDK standard.
Max timecode scale value length	1 second	The maximum timecode scale value to represent the frame time stamps in the resulting MKV cluster. The value is specified in increments of 100 ns, which is the SDK standard.
Min content view item count	10	
Min buffer duration	20 seconds	The value is specified in increments of 100 ns, which is the SDK standard.
Max update version length	128 characters	
Max ARN length	1024 characters	
Max fragment sequence length	128 characters	
Max retention period	10 years	

Error Code Reference

This section contains error and status code information for the Producer Libraries.

For information about solutions to common issues, see Troubleshooting Kinesis Video Streams.

Errors and Status Codes Returned by PutFrame Callbacks

The following sections contain error and status information that is returned by callbacks for the `PutFrame` operation.

Topics

- Error and Status Codes Returned by the Client Library
- Error and Status Codes Returned by the Duration Library
- Error and Status Codes Returned by the Common Library
- Error and Status Codes Returned by the Heap Library
- Error and Status Codes Returned by the MKVGen Library
- Error and Status Codes Returned by the Trace Library
- Error and Status Codes Returned by the Utils Library
- Error and Status Codes Returned by the View Library

Error and Status Codes Returned by the Client Library

The following table contains error and status information that is returned by methods in the Kinesis Video Streams `Client` library.

Code	Message	Description	Recommended Action
0x52000001	STATUS_MAX_STREAM_	The maximum stream count was reached.	Specify a larger max stream count in DeviceInfo as specified in Producer SDK Limits.
0x52000002	STATUS_MIN_STREAM_	Minimum stream count error.	Specify the max number of streams greater than 0 in DeviceInfo.
0x52000003	STATUS_INVALID_DEVICE_NAME_LENGT	Invalid device name length.	Refer to the max device name length in characters that is specified in Producer SDK Limits.
0x52000004	STATUS_INVALID_DEVICE_INFO_VERSION	Invalid DeviceInfo structure version.	Specify the correct current version of the structure.
0x52000005	STATUS_MAX_TAG_COⁱ	The maximum tag count was reached.	Refer to the current max tag count that is specified in Producer SDK Limits.
0x52000006	STATUS_DEVICE_FINGERPRINT_LENGTH		

Code	Message	Description	Recommended Action
0x52000007	STATUS_IN-VALID_CALL-BACKS_VERSION	Invalid Callbacks structure version.	Specify the correct current version of the structure.
0x52000008	STATUS_IN-VALID_STREAM_INF SION	Invalid StreamInfo structure version.	Specify the correct current version of the structure.
0x52000009	STATUS_IN-VALID_STREAM_NA	Invalid stream name length.	Refer to the max stream name length in characters that is specified in Producer SDK Limits.
0x5200000a	STATUS_IN-VALID_STOR-AGE_SIZE	An invalid storage size was specified.	The storage size in bytes must be within the limits specified in Producer SDK Limits.
0x5200000b	STATUS_IN-VALID_ROOT_DI-REC-TORY_LENGTH	Invalid root directory string length.	Refer to the max root directory path length that is specified in Producer SDK Limits.
0x5200000c	STATUS_IN-VALID_SPILL_RA-TIO	Invalid spill ratio.	Express the spill ratio as a percentage from 0 to 100.
0x5200000d	STATUS_IN-VALID_STOR-AGE_INFO_VER-SION	Invalid StorageInfo structure version.	Specify the correct current version of the structure.
0x5200000e	STATUS_IN-VALID_STREAM_ST/	The stream is in a state that doesn't permit the current operation.	Most commonly, this error occurs when the SDK fails to reach the state that it needs to perform the requested operation. For example, it occurs if the GetStreamingEndpoint API call fails, and the client application ignores it and continues putting frames into the stream.
0x5200000f	STATUS_SER-VICE_CALL_CALL-BACKS_MISSING	The Callbacks structure has missing function entry points for some mandatory functions.	Ensure that the mandatory callbacks are implemented in the client application. This error is exposed only to PIC (Platform Independent Code) clients. C++ and other higher-level wrappers satisfy these calls.

Code	Message	Description	Recommended Action
0x52000010	STATUS_SER-VICE_CALL_NOT_A THORIZED_ERROR	Not authorized.	Verify the security token/certificate/security token integration/-expiration. Ensure that the token has the correct associated rights with it. For the Kinesis Video Streams sample applications, ensure that the environment variable is set correctly.
0x52000011	STATUS_DE-SCRIBE_STREAM_C.	DescribeStream API failure.	This error is returned after the Describe-Stream API retry failure. The PIC client returns this error after it gives up retrying.
0x52000012	STATUS_IN-VALID_DE-SCRIBE_STREAM_R. SPONSE	Invalid Describe-StreamResponse structure.	The structure that was passed to the Describe-StreamResultEvent is either null or contains invalid items like a null Amazon Resource Name (ARN).
0x52000013	STA-TUS_STREAM_IS_BI ING_DELETED_ER-ROR	The stream is being deleted.	An API failure was caused by the stream being deleted. Ensure that no other processes are trying to delete the stream while the stream is in use.
0x52000014	STATUS_SER-VICE_CALL_IN-VALID_ARG_ER-ROR	Invalid arguments were specified for the service call.	The backend returns this error when a service call argument is not valid or when the SDK encounters an error that it can't interpret.
0x52000015	STATUS_SER-VICE_CALL_DE-VICE_NOT_FOUND_ ROR	The device was not found.	Ensure that the device is not deleted while in use.
0x52000016	STATUS_SER-VICE_CALL_DE-VICE_NOT_PROVI-SIONED_ERROR	The device was not provisioned.	Ensure that the device has been provisioned.

Code	Message	Description	Recommended Action
0x52000017	STATUS_SER-VICE_CALL_RE-SOURCE_NOT_FOUN ROR	Generic resource not found returned from the service.	This error occurs when the service can't locate the resource (for example, a stream). It might mean different things in different contexts, but the likely cause is the usage of APIs before the stream is created. Using the SDK ensures that the stream is created first.
0x52000018	STATUS_IN-VALID_AUTH_LEN	Invalid auth info length.	Refer to the current values that are specified in Producer SDK Limits.
0x52000019	STATUS_CRE-ATE_STREAM_CALL	The CreateStream API call failed.	Refer to the error string for more detailed information about why the operation failed.
0x5200002a	STA-TUS_GET_STREAM-ING_TO-KEN_CALL_FAILED	The GetStreamingTo-ken call failed.	Refer to the error string for more detailed information about why the operation failed.
0x5200002b	STA-TUS_GET_STREAM-ING_END-POINT_CALL_FAILE	The GetStreamin-gEndpoint API call failed.	Refer to the error string for more detailed information about why the operation failed.
0x5200002c	STATUS_IN-VALID_URI_LEN	An invalid URI string length was returned from the GetStreamin-gEndpoint API.	Refer to the current maximum values that are specified in Producer SDK Limits.
0x5200002d	STA-TUS_PUT_STREAM_	The PutMedia API call failed.	Refer to the error string for more detailed information about why the operation failed.

Code	Message	Description	Recommended Action
0x5200002e	STA-TUS_STORE_OUT_C ORY	The content store is out of memory.	The content store is shared between the streams and should have enough capacity to store the maximum durations for all the streams + ~20% (accounting for the defragmentation). It's important to not overflow the storage. Choose values for the maximum duration per stream that correspond to the cumulative storage size and the latency tolerances. It's better to drop the frames as they fall out of the content view window versus just being put (content store memory pressure). This is because dropping the frames triggers the stream pressure notification callbacks. Then the application can adjust the upstream media components (like the encoder) to thin the bitrate, drop frames, or act accordingly.
0x5200002f	STA-TUS_NO_MORE_DA ABLE	No more data is available currently for a stream.	This is a potential valid result when the media pipeline produces more slowly than the networking thread consumes the frames to be sent to the service. Higher-level clients (for example, C++, Java, or Android) do not see this warning because it's handled internally.
0x52000030	STATUS_IN-VALID_TAG_VER-SION	Invalid Tag structure version.	Specify the correct current version of the structure.

Code	Message	Description	Recommended Action
0x52000031	STATUS_SER-VICE_CALL_UN-KOWN_ERROR	An unknown or generic error was returned from the networking stack.	See the logs for more detailed information.
0x52000032	STATUS_SER-VICE_CALL_RE-SOURCE_IN_USE_EI ROR	Resource in use.	Returned from the service. For more information, see the Kinesis Video Streams API Reference.
0x52000033	STATUS_SER-VICE_CALL_CLIENT ROR	Client limit.	Returned from the service. For more information, see the Kinesis Video Streams API Reference.
0x52000034	STATUS_SER-VICE_CALL_DE-VICE_LIMIT_ER-ROR	Device limit.	Returned from the service. For more information, see the Kinesis Video Streams API Reference.
0x52000035	STATUS_SER-VICE_CALL_STREAN ROR	Stream limit.	Returned from the service. For more information, see the Kinesis Video Streams API Reference.
0x52000036	STATUS_SER-VICE_CALL_RE-SOURCE_DELETED_ ROR	The resource was deleted or is being deleted.	Returned from the service. For more information, see the Kinesis Video Streams API Reference.
0x52000037	STATUS_SER-VICE_CALL_TIME-OUT_ERROR	The service call timed out.	Calling a particular service API resulted in a timeout. Ensure that you have a valid network connection. The PIC will retry the operation automatically.
0x52000038	STA-TUS_STREAM_REAI BACK_FAILED	Stream ready notification.	This notification is sent from the PIC to the client indicating that the async stream has been created.
0x52000039	STATUS_DE-VICE_TAGS_COUNT	Invalid tags were specified.	The tag count is not zero, but the tags are empty. Ensure that the tags are specified or the count is zero.
0x5200003a	STATUS_IN-VALID_STREAM_DE SCRIPTION_VER-SION	Invalid StreamDescription structure version.	Specify the correct current version of the structure.

Code	Message	Description	Recommended Action
0x5200003b	STATUS_IN-VALID_TAG_NAME_	Invalid tag name length.	Refer to the limits for the tag name that are specified in Producer SDK Limits.
0x5200003c	STATUS_IN-VALID_TAG_VALUE_	Invalid tag value length.	Refer to the limits for the tag value that are specified in Producer SDK Limits.
0x5200003d	STA-TUS_TAG_STREAM_	The TagResource API failed.	The TagResource API call failed. Check for a valid network connection. See the logs for more information about the failure.
0x5200003e	STATUS_IN-VALID_CUS-TOM_DATA	Invalid custom data calling PIC APIs.	Invalid custom data has been specified in a call to the PIC APIs. This can occur only in the clients that directly use PIC.
0x5200003f	STATUS_IN-VALID_CRE-ATE_STREAM_RE-SPONSE	Invalid CreateStream-Response structure.	The structure or its member fields are invalid (that is, the ARN is null or larger than what's specified in Producer SDK Limits).
0x52000040	STA-TUS_CLIENT_AUTH_	Client auth failed.	The PIC failed to get proper auth information (that is, AccessKeyId or SecretAccessKey) after a number of retries. Check the authentication integration. The sample applications use environment variables to pass in credential information to the C++ Producer Library.
0x52000041	STA-TUS_GET_CLIENT_'KEN_CALL_FAILED	Getting the security token call failed.	This situation can occur for clients that use PIC directly. After a number of retries, the call fails with this error.
0x52000042	STA-TUS_CLIENT_PRO-VI-SION_CALL_FAILED	Provisioning error.	Provisioning is not implemented.

Code	Message	Description	Recommended Action
0x52000043	STATUS_CRE-ATE_CLIENT_CALL_	Failed to create the producer client.	A generic error returned by the PIC after a number of retries when the client creation fails.
0x52000044	STA-TUS_CLIENT_READ`BACK_FAILED	Failed to get the producer client to a READY state.	Returned by the PIC state machine if the PIC fails to move to the READY state. See the logs for more information about the root cause.
0x52000045	STA-TUS_TAG_CLIENT_(	The TagResource for the producer client failed.	The TagResource API call failed for the producer client. See the logs for more information about the root cause.
0x52000046	STATUS_IN-VALID_CRE-ATE_DEVICE_RE-SPONSE	Device/Producer creation failed.	The higher-level SDKs (for example, C++ or Java) don't implement the device/producer creation API yet. Clients that use PIC directly can indicate a failure using the result notification.
0x52000047	STA-TUS_ACK_TIMES-TAMP_NOT_IN_VIE`DOW	The time stamp of the received ACK is not in the view.	This error occurs if the frame corresponding to the received ACK falls out of the content view window. Generally, this occurs if the ACK delivery is slow. It can be interpreted as a warning and an indication that the downlink is slow.
0x52000048	STATUS_IN-VALID_FRAG-MENT_ACK_VER-SION	Invalid FragmentAck structure version.	Specify the correct current version of the FragmentAck structure.
0x52000049	STATUS_IN-VALID_TO-KEN_EXPIRATION	Invalid security token expiration.	The security token expiration should have an absolute time stamp in the future that is greater than the current time stamp, with a grace period. For the limits for the grace period, see the Producer SDK Limits.

Code	Message	Description	Recommended Action
0x5200004a	STATUS_END_OF_STRE	End of stream (EOS) indicator.	In the GetStreamData API call, indicates that the current upload handle session has ended. This occurs if the session ends or errors, or if the session token has expired and the session is being rotated.
0x5200004b	STATUS_DUPLICATE_STREAM_NAI	Duplicate stream name.	Multiple streams can't have the same stream name. Choose a unique name for the stream.
0x5200004c	STATUS_INVALID_RETENTION_PERIOD	Invalid retention period.	An invalid retention period is specified in the StreamInfo structure. For information about the valid range of values for the retention period, see Producer SDK Limits.
0x5200004d	STATUS_INVALID_ACK_KEY_S'	Invalid FragmentAck.	Failed to parse the fragment ACK string. Invalid key start indicator. The fragment ACK string might be damaged. It can self-correct and this error can be treated as a warning.
0x5200004e	STATUS_INVALID_ACK_DUPLICATE_KEY_NAME	Invalid FragmentAck.	Failed to parse the fragment ACK string. Multiple keys have the same name. The fragment ACK string might be damaged. It can self-correct and this error can be treated as a warning.
0x5200004f	STATUS_INVALID_ACK_INVALID_VALUE_STAF	Invalid FragmentAck.	Failed to parse the fragment ACK string because of an invalid key value start indicator. The fragment ACK string might be damaged. It can self-correct, and this error can be treated as a warning.

Code	Message	Description	Recommended Action
0x52000050	STATUS_IN-VALID_ACK_IN-VALID_VALUE_END	Invalid FragmentAck.	Failed to parse the fragment ACK string because of an invalid key value end indicator. The fragment ACK string might be damaged. It can self-correct and this error can be treated as a warning.
0x52000051	STATUS_IN-VALID_PARSED_ACI	Invalid FragmentAck.	Failed to parse the fragment ACK string because an invalid ACK type was specified.
0x52000052	STA-TUS_STREAM_HAS_	Stream was stopped.	The stream has been stopped, but a frame is still being put into the stream.
0x52000053	STATUS_IN-VALID_STREAM_ME RICS_VERSION	Invalid StreamMetrics structure version.	Specify the correct current version of the StreamMetrics structure.
0x52000054	STATUS_IN-VALID_CLIENT_MET RICS_VERSION	Invalid ClientMetrics structure version.	Specify the correct current version of the ClientMetrics structure.
0x52000055	STATUS_IN-VALID_CLIENT_REA	Producer initialization failed to reach a READY state.	Failed to reach the READY state during the producer client initialization. See the logs for more information.
0x52000056	STA-TUS_STATE_MA-CHINE_STATE_NOT	Internal state machine error.	Not a publicly visible error.
0x52000057	STATUS_IN-VALID_FRAG-MENT_ACK_TYPE	Invalid ACK type is specified in the FragmentAck structure.	The FragmentAck structure should contain ACK types defined in the public header.
0x52000058	STATUS_IN-VALID_STREAM_RE	Internal state machine transition error.	Not a publicly visible error.
0x52000059	STA-TUS_CLIENT_FREEI FORE_STREAM	The stream object was freed after the producer was freed.	There was an attempt to free a stream object after the producer object was freed. This can only occur in clients that directly use PIC.

Code	Message	Description	Recommended Action
0x5200005a	STATUS_ALLOCA-TION_SIZE_SMALLE QUESTED	Internal storage error.	An internal error indicating that the actual allocation size from the content store is smaller than the size of the packaged frame/fragment.
0x5200005b	STA-TUS_VIEW_ITEM_S LOCATION	Internal storage error.	The stored size of the allocation in the content view is greater than the allocation size in the content store.
0x5200005c	STA-TUS_ACK_ERR_STR ROR	Stream read error ACK.	An error that the ACK returned from the backend indicating a stream read/parsing error. This generally occurs when the backend fails to retrieve the stream. Auto-restreaming can usually correct this error.
0x5200005d	STA-TUS_ACK_ERR_FR MENT_SIZE_REACH	The maximum fragment size was reached.	The max fragment size in bytes is defined in Producer SDK Limits. This error indicates that there are either very large frames, or there are no key frames to create manageable size fragments. Check the encoder settings and ensure that key frames are being produced properly. For streams that have very high density, configure the encoder to produce fragments at smaller durations to manage the maximum size.

Code	Message	Description	Recommended Action
0x5200005e	STA-TUS_ACK_ERR_FRAMENT_DURA-TION_REACHED	The maximum fragment duration was reached.	The max fragment duration is defined in Producer SDK Limits. This error indicates that there are either very low frames per second or there are no key frames to create manageable duration fragments. Check the encoder settings and ensure that key frames are being produced properly at the regular intervals.
0x5200005f	STA-TUS_ACK_ERR_CONNECTION_DURA-TION_REACHED	The maximum connection duration was reached.	Kinesis Video Streams enforces the max connection duration as specified in the Producer SDK Limits. The Producer SDK automatically rotates the stream/token before the maximum is reached, and so clients using the SDK should not receive this error.
0x52000060	STA-TUS_ACK_ERR_FRAMENT_TIME-CODE_NOT_MONO-TONIC	Timecodes are not monotonically increasing.	The Producer SDK enforces time stamps, so clients using the SDK should not receive this error.
0x52000061	STA-TUS_ACK_ERR_MUI	Multiple tracks in the MKV.	The Producer SDK enforces single track streams, so clients using the SDK should not receive this error.

Code	Message	Description	Recommended Action
0x52000062	STATUS_ACK_ERR_INVALID_MKV_DATA	Invalid MKV data.	The backend MKV parser encountered an error parsing the stream. Clients using the SDK might encounter this error if the stream is corrupted in the transition or if the buffer pressures force the SDK to drop tail frames that are partially transmitted. In the latter case, we recommend that you either reduce the FPS/resolution, increase the compression ratio, or (in the case of a "bursty" network) allow for larger content store and buffer duration to accommodate for the temporary pressures.
0x52000063	STATUS_ACK_ERR_INVALID_PRODUCER_TIMESTAMP	Invalid producer time stamp.	The service returns this error ACK if the producer clock has a large drift into the future. Higher-level SDKs (for example, Java or C++) use some version of the system clock to satisfy the current time callback from PIC. Ensure that the system clock is set properly. Clients using the PIC directly should ensure that their callback functions return the correct time stamp.

Code	Message	Description	Recommended Action
0x52000064	STATUS_ACK_ERR_STR TIVE	Inactive stream.	A call to a backend API was made while the stream was not in an "Active" state. This occurs when the client creates the stream and immediately continues to push frames into it. The SDK handles this scenario through the state machine and recovery mechanism.
0x52000065	STATUS_ACK_ERR_KM! CESS_DENIED	AWS KMS access denied error.	Returned when the account has no access to the specified key.
0x52000066	STATUS_ACK_ERR_KM! ABLED	AWS KMS key is disabled	The specified key has been disabled.
0x52000067	STATUS_ACK_ERR_KM! IDATION_ERROR	AWS KMS key validation error.	Generic validation error. For more information, see the AWS Key Management Service API Reference.
0x52000068	STATUS_ACK_ERR_KM! AVAILABLE	AWS KMS key unavailable.	The key is unavailable. For more information, see the AWS Key Management Service API Reference.
0x52000069	STATUS_ACK_ERR_KM! VALID_USAGE	Invalid use of AWS KMS key.	The AWS KMS key is not configured to be used in this context. For more information, see the AWS Key Management Service API Reference.
0x5200006a	STATUS_ACK_ERR_KM! VALID_STATE	AWS KMS invalid state.	For more information, see the AWS Key Management Service API Reference.
0x5200006b	STATUS_ACK_ERR_KM!	AWS KMS key not found.	The key was not found. For more information, see the AWS Key Management Service API Reference.
0x5200006c	STATUS_ACK_ERR_STR	The stream has been or is being deleted.	The stream is being deleted by another application or through the AWS Management Console.
0x5200006d	STATUS_ACK_ERR_ACF TERNAL_ERROR	Internal error.	Generic service internal error.

Code	Message	Description	Recommended Action
0x5200006e	STA-TUS_ACK_ERR_FRA MENT_ARCHIVAL_E ROR	Fragment archival error.	Returned when the service fails to durably persist and index the fragment. Although it's rare, it can occur for various reasons. By default, the SDK retries sending the fragment.
0x5200006f	STA-TUS_ACK_ERR_UN-KNOWN_ACK_ER-ROR	Unknown error.	The service returned an unknown error.
0x52000070	STATUS_MISS-ING_ERR_ACK_ID	Missing ACK information.	The ACK parser completed parsing, but the FragmentAck information is missing.
0x52000071	STATUS_IN-VALID_ACK_SEG-MENT_LEN	Invalid ACK segment length.	An ACK segment string with an invalid length was specified to the ACK parser. For more information, see Producer SDK Limits.

Error and Status Codes Returned by the Duration Library

The following table contains error and status information that is returned by methods in the **Duration** library.

Code	Message
0xFFFFFFFFFFFFFFFF	INVALID_DURATION_VALUE

Error and Status Codes Returned by the Common Library

The following table contains error and status information that is returned by methods in the **Common** library.

Note
These error and status information codes are common to many APIs.

Code	Message	Description
0x00000001	STATUS_NULL_ARG	NULL was passed for a mandatory argument.
0x00000002	STATUS_INVALID_ARG	An invalid value was specified for an argument.
0x00000003	STATUS_IN-VALID_ARG_LEN	An invalid argument length was specified.
0x00000004	STA-TUS_NOT_ENOUGH_MEM-ORY	Could not allocate enough memory.

82

Code	Message	Description
0x00000005	STA-TUS_BUFFER_TOO_SMALL	The specified buffer size is too small.
0x00000006	STATUS_UNEX-PECTED_EOF	An unexpected end of file was reached.
0x00000007	STATUS_FORMAT_ER-ROR	An invalid format was encountered.
0x00000008	STATUS_INVALID_HAN-DLE_ERROR	Invalid handle value.
0x00000009	STA-TUS_OPEN_FILE_FAILED	Failed to open a file.
0x0000000a	STA-TUS_READ_FILE_FAILED	Failed to read from a file.
0x0000000b	STA-TUS_WRITE_TO_FILE_FAI	Failed to write to a file.
0x0000000c	STATUS_INTERNAL_ER-ROR	An internal error that normally doesn't occur and might indicate an SDK or service API bug.
0x0000000d	STATUS_INVALID_OPER-ATION	There was an invalid operation, or the operation is not permitted.
0x0000000e	STATUS_NOT_IMPLE-MENTED	The feature is not implemented.
0x0000000f	STATUS_OPERA-TION_TIMED_OUT	The operation timed out.
0x00000010	STATUS_NOT_FOUND	A required resource was not found.

Error and Status Codes Returned by the Heap Library

The following table contains error and status information that is returned by methods in the **Heap** library.

Code	Message	Description
0x01000001	STA-TUS_HEAP_FLAGS_ER-ROR	An invalid combination of flags was specified.
0x01000002	STATUS_HEAP_NOT_INI-TIALIZED	An operation was attempted before the heap was initialized.
0x01000003	STATUS_HEAP_COR-RUPTED	The heap was corrupted or the guard band (in debug mode) was overwritten. A buffer overflow in the client code might lead to a heap corruption.
0x01000004	STA-TUS_HEAP_VRAM_LIB_MI ING	The VRAM (video RAM) user or kernel mode library cannot be loaded or is missing. Check if the underlying platform supports VRAM allocations.

Code	Message	Description
0x01000005	STATUS_HEAP_VRAM_LIB_RE_OPEN	Failed to open the VRAM library.
0x01000006	STATUS_HEAP_VRAM_INIT_F BOL	Failed to load the INIT function export.
0x01000007	STATUS_HEAP_VRAM_ALLOC_FUNC_SYMBOL	Failed to load the ALLOC function export.
0x01000008	STATUS_HEAP_VRAM_FREE_ BOL	Failed to load the FREE function export.
0x01000009	STATUS_HEAP_VRAM_LOCK_ BOL	Failed to load the LOCK function export.
0x0100000a	STATUS_HEAP_VRAM_UNLOCK_FUNC_SYMBOL	Failed to load the UNLOCK function export.
0x0100000b	STATUS_HEAP_VRAM_UNINIT BOL	Failed to load the UNINIT function export.
0x0100000c	STATUS_HEAP_VRAM_GETMAX_FUNC_SYMBOL	Failed to load the GETMAX function export.
0x0100000d	STATUS_HEAP_DIRECT_MEM_INIT	Failed to initialize the main heap pool in the hybrid heap.
0x0100000e	STATUS_HEAP_VRAM_INIT_F	The VRAM dynamic initialization failed.
0x0100000f	STATUS_HEAP_LIBRARY_FREE_FAILED	Failed to de-allocate and free the VRAM library.
0x01000010	STATUS_HEAP_VRAM_ALLOC_FAILED	The VRAM allocation failed.
0x01000011	STATUS_HEAP_VRAM_FREE_	The VRAM free failed.
0x01000012	STATUS_HEAP_VRAM_MAP_F	The VRAM map failed.
0x01000013	STATUS_HEAP_VRAM_UNMAP_FAILED	The VRAM unmap failed.
0x01000014	STATUS_HEAP_VRAM_UNINIT	The VRAM deinitialization failed.

Error and Status Codes Returned by the MKVGen Library

The following table contains error and status information that is returned by methods in the MKVGen library.

Code	Message	Description / Recommended Action
0x32000001	STATUS_MKV_IN-VALID_FRAME_DATA	Invalid members of the Frame data structure. Ensure that the duration, size, and frame data are valid and are within the limits specified in Producer SDK Limits.
0x32000002	STATUS_MKV_IN-VALID_FRAME_TIMES-TAMP	Invalid frame time stamp. The calculated PTS (presentation time stamp) and DTS (decoding time stamp) are greater or equal to the time stamp of the start frame of the fragment. This is an indication of a potential media pipeline restart or an encoder stability issue. For troubleshooting information, see Error: "Failed to submit frame to Kinesis Video client"
0x32000003	STATUS_MKV_IN-VALID_CLUSTER_DU-RATION	An invalid fragment duration was specified. For more information, see Producer SDK Limits.
0x32000004	STATUS_MKV_IN-VALID_CON-TENT_TYPE_LENGTH	Invalid content type string length. For more information, see Producer SDK Limits.
0x32000005	STATUS_MKV_NUM-BER_TOO_BIG	There was an attempt to encode a number that's too large to be represented in EBML (Extensible Binary Meta Language) format. This should not be exposed to the SDK clients.
0x32000006	STATUS_MKV_IN-VALID_CODEC_ID_LENGT	Invalid codec ID string length. For more information, see Producer SDK Limits.
0x32000007	STATUS_MKV_IN-VALID_TRACK_NAME_LEN	Invalid track name string length. For more information, see Producer SDK Limits.
0x32000008	STATUS_MKV_IN-VALID_CODEC_PRI-VATE_LENGTH	Invalid codec private data length. For more information, see Producer SDK Limits.
0x32000009	STA-TUS_MKV_CODEC_PRI-VATE_NULL	The codec private data (CPD) is NULL, whereas the CPD size is greater than 0.
0x3200000a	STATUS_MKV_IN-VALID_TIME-CODE_SCALE	Invalid timecode scale value. For more information, see Producer SDK Limits.
0x3200000b	STA-TUS_MKV_MAX_FRAME_CODE	The frame timecode is greater than the maximum. For more information, see Producer SDK Limits.

Code	Message	Description / Recommended Action
0x3200000c	STATUS_MKV_LARGE_FRAME CODE	The max frame timecode was reached. The MKV format uses signed 16 bits to represent the relative timecode of the frame to the beginning of the cluster. The error is generated if the frame timecode cannot be represented. This error indicates either a bad timecode scale selection or the cluster duration is too long, so representing the frame timecode overflows the signed 16-bit space.
0x3200000d	STATUS_MKV_IN-VALID_AN-NEXB_NALU_IN_FRAME_	An invalid Annex-B start code was encountered. For example, the Annex-B adaptation flag was specified and the code encounters an invalid start sequence of more than three zeroes. A valid Annex-B format should have an "emulation prevention" sequence to escape a sequence of three or more zeroes in the bytestream. For more information, see the MPEG specification.
0x3200000e	STATUS_MKV_IN-VALID_AVCC_NALU_IN_FI	Invalid AVCC NALu packaging when the adapting AVCC flag is specified. Ensure that the bytestream is in a valid AVCC format. For more information, see the MPEG specification.
0x3200000f	STATUS_MKV_BOTH_AN-NEXB_AND_AVCC_SPEC-IFIED	Both adapting AVCC and Annex-B NALs were specified. Specify either one, or specify none.
0x32000010	STATUS_MKV_IN-VALID_AN-NEXB_NALU_IN_CPD	Invalid Annex-B format of CPD when the adapting Annex-B flag is specified. Ensure that the CPD is in valid Annex-B format. If it is not, then remove the CPD Annex-B adaptation flag.

Code	Message	Description / Recommended Action
0x32000011	STA-TUS_MKV_PTS_DTS_ARE_	Kinesis Video Streams enforces the PTS (presentation time stamp) and DTS (decoding time stamp) to be the same for the fragment start frames. These are the key frames that start the fragment.
0x32000012	STATUS_MKV_IN-VALID_H264_H265_CPD	Failed to parse H264/H265 codec private data.
0x32000013	STATUS_MKV_IN-VALID_H264_H265_SPS_WI	Failed to extract the width from the codec private data.
0x32000014	STATUS_MKV_IN-VALID_H264_H265_SPS_HE	Failed to extract the height from codec private data.
0x32000015	STATUS_MKV_IN-VALID_H264_H265_SPS_NA	Invalid H264/H265 SPS NALu.
0x32000016	STATUS_MKV_IN-VALID_BIH_CPD	Invalid bitmap info header format in the codec private data.

Error and Status Codes Returned by the Trace Library

The following table contains error and status information that is returned by methods in the `Trace` library.

Code	Message
0x10100001	STATUS_MIN_PROFILER_BUFFER

Error and Status Codes Returned by the Utils Library

The following table contains error and status information that is returned by methods in the `Utils` library.

Code	Message
0x40000001	STATUS_INVALID_BASE64_ENCODE
0x40000002	STATUS_INVALID_BASE
0x40000003	STATUS_INVALID_DIGIT
0x40000004	STATUS_INT_OVERFLOW
0x40000005	STATUS_EMPTY_STRING
0x40000006	STATUS_DIRECTORY_OPEN_FAILED
0x40000007	STATUS_PATH_TOO_LONG
0x40000008	STATUS_UNKNOWN_DIR_EN-TRY_TYPE
0x40000009	STATUS_REMOVE_DIREC-TORY_FAILED
0x4000000a	STATUS_REMOVE_FILE_FAILED
0x4000000b	STATUS_REMOVE_LINK_FAILED
0x4000000c	STATUS_DIRECTORY_ACCESS_DE-NIED

Code	Message
0x4000000d	STATUS_DIRECTORY_MISSING_PATH
0x4000000e	STATUS_DIRECTORY_EN-TRY_STAT_ERROR

Error and Status Codes Returned by the View Library

The following table contains error and status information that is returned by methods in the View library.

Code	Message	Description
0x30000001	STATUS_MIN_CON-TENT_VIEW_ITEMS	An invalid content view item count was specified. For more information, see Producer SDK Limits.
0x30000002	STATUS_INVALID_CON-TENT_VIEW_DURATION	An invalid content view duration was specified. For more information, see Producer SDK Limits.
0x30000003	STATUS_CON-TENT_VIEW_NO_MORE_I'	An attempt was made to get past the head position.
0x30000004	STATUS_CON-TENT_VIEW_IN-VALID_INDEX	An invalid index is specified.

Code	Message	Description
0x30000005	STATUS_CONTENT_VIEW_INVALID_TIMESTAMP	There was an invalid time stamp or a time stamp overlap. The frame decoding time stamp should be greater or equal to the previous frame time stamp, plus the previous frame duration: DTS\(n\) >= DTS\(n\-1\) \+ Duration\(n\-1\). This error often indicates an "unstable" encoder. The encoder produces a burst of encoded frames, and their time stamps are smaller than the intra-frame durations. Or the stream is configured to use SDK time stamps, and the frames are sent faster than the frame durations. To help with some "jitter" in the encoder, specify a smaller frame duration in the StreamInfo.StreamCaps structure. For example, if the stream is 25FPS, each frame's duration is 40 ms. However, to handle the encoder jitter, we recommend that you use half of that frame duration (20 ms). Some streams require more precise control over the timing for error detection.
0x30000006	STATUS_INVALID_CONTENT_VIEW_LENGTH	An invalid content view item data length was specified.

Network Abstraction Layer (NAL) Adaptation Flag Reference

This section contains information about available flags for the `StreamInfo.NalAdaptationFlags` enumeration.

The elementary stream in an application can be in either **Annex-B** or **AVCC** format:

- The **Annex-B** format delimits NALUs (Network Abstraction Layer units) with two bytes of zeroes, followed by one or three bytes of zeroes, followed by the number *1* (called a **start code**, for example, 00000001).
- The **AVCC** format also wraps NALUs, but each NALU is preceded by a value that indicates the size of the NALU (usually four bytes).

Many encoders produce the Annex-B bitstream format. Some higher-level bitstream processors (such as a playback engine or the Media Source Extensions (MSE) player in the AWS Management Console) use the AVCC format for their frames.

The codec private data (CPD), which is SPS/PPS (Sequence Parameter Set/Picture Parameter Set) for the H.264 codec, can also be in Annex-B or AVCC format. However, for the CPD, the formats are different from those described previously.

The flags tell the SDK to adapt the NALUs to AVCC or Annex-B for frame data and CPD as follows:

Flag	Adaptation
NAL_ADAPTATION_FLAG_NONE	No adaptation
NAL_ADAPTATION_ANNEXB_NALS	Adapt Annex-B NALUs to AVCC NALUs
NAL_ADAPTATION_AVCC_NALS	Adapt AVCC NALUs to Annex-B NALUs
NAL_ADAPTATION_AN-NEXB_CPD_NALS	Adapt Annex-B NALUs for the codec private data to AVCC format NALUs
NAL_ADAPTATION_AN-NEXB_CPD_AND_FRAME_NALS	Adapt Annex-B NALUs for the codec and frame private data to AVCC format NALUs

For more information about NALU types, see **Section 1.3: Network Abstraction Layer Unit Types** in RFC 3984.

Producer SDK Structures

This section includes information about structures that you can use to provide data to the Kinesis Video Streams Producer object.

Topics

- DeviceInfo/DefaultDeviceInfoProvider
- StorageInfo

DeviceInfo/DefaultDeviceInfoProvider

The **DeviceInfo** and **DevaultDeviceInfoProvider** objects control the behavior of the Kinesis Video Streams Producer object.

Member Fields

- **version**: An integer value used to ensure that the correct version of the structure is used with the current version of the code base. The current version is specified using the `DEVICE_INFO_CURRENT_VERSION` macro.
- **name**: The human-readable name for the device.
- **tagCount/tags**: Not currently used.
- **streamCount**: The maximum number of streams that the device can handle. This pre-allocates the storage for pointers to the stream objects initially, but the actual stream objects are created later. The default is 16 streams, but you can change this number in the `DefaultDeviceInfoProvider.cpp` file.
- **storageInfo**: An object that describes the main storage configuration. For more information, see StorageInfo.

StorageInfo

Specifies the configuration of the main storage for Kinesis Video Streams.

The default implementation is based on a low-fragmentation fast heap implementation, which is optimized for streaming. It uses the `MEMALLOC` allocator, which can be overwritten on a given platform. Some platforms have virtual memory allocation without backing the allocation with physical pages. As the memory is used, the virtual pages are backed by the physical pages. This results in low-memory pressure on the overall system when storage is underused.

Calculate the default storage size based on the following formula. The `DefragmentationFactor` should be set to 1.2 (20 percent).

```
1 Size = NumberOfStreams * AverageFrameSize * FramesPerSecond * BufferDurationInSeconds *
     DefragmentationFactor
```

In the following example, a device has audio and video streams. The audio stream has 512 samples per second, with an average sample of 100 bytes. The video stream has 25 frames per second, with an average of 10,000 bytes. Each stream has 3 minutes of buffer duration.

```
1 Size = (512 * 100 * (3 * 60) + 25 * 10000 * (3 * 60)) * 1.2 = (9216000 + 45000000) * 1.2 =
     65059200 = ~ 66MB.
```

If the device has more available memory, it is recommended that you add more memory to storage to avoid severe fragmentation.

Ensure that the storage size is adequate to accommodate the full buffers for all streams at high encoding complexity (when the frame size is larger due to high motion) or when the bandwidth is low. If the producer hits memory pressure, it emits storage overflow pressure callbacks (`StorageOverflowPressureFunc`). However, when no memory is available in the content store, it drops the frame that's being pushed into Kinesis Video Streams with an error (`STATUS_STORE_OUT_OF_MEMORY = 0x5200002e`). For more information, see Error and Status Codes Returned by the Client Library. This can also happen if the application acknowledgements (ACKs) are not available, or the persisted ACKs are delayed. In this case, the buffers fill to the "buffer duration" capacity before the older frames start dropping out.

Member Fields

- **version**: An integer value used to ensure that the correct version of the structure is used with the current version of the code base.
- **storageType**: A `DEVICE_STORAGE_TYPE` enumeration that specifies the underlying backing/implementation of the storage. Currently the only supported value is `DEVICE_STORAGE_TYPE_IN_MEM`. A future implementation will support `DEVICE_STORAGE_TYPE_HYBRID_FILE`, indicating that storage falls back to the file-backed content store.
- **storageSize**: The storage size in bytes to preallocate. The minimum allocation is 10 MB, and the maximum allocation is 10 GB. (This will change with the future implementation of the file-backed content store.)
- **spillRatio**: An integer value that represents the percentage of the storage to be allocated from the direct memory storage type (RAM), as opposed to the secondary overflow storage (file storage). Not currently used.
- **rootDirectory**: The path to the directory where the file-backed content store is located. Not currently used.

Kinesis Video Stream Structures

You can use the following structures to provide data to an instance of a Kinesis video stream.

Topics

- StreamDefinition/ StreamInfo
- ClientMetrics
- StreamMetrics

StreamDefinition/ StreamInfo

The `StreamDefinition` object in the C++ layer wraps the `StreamInfo` object in the platform-independent code, and provides some default values in the constructor.

Member Fields

Field	Data Type	Description	Default Value
stream_name	string	An optional stream name. For more information about the length of the stream name, see Producer SDK Limits . Each stream should have a unique name.	If no name is specified, a name is generated randomly.
retention_period	duration<uint64_t, ratio<3600»	The retention period for the stream, in seconds. Specifying 0 indicates no retention.	3600 (One hour)
tags	const map<string, string>*	A map of key-value pairs that contain user information. If the stream already has a set of tags, the new tags are appended to the existing set of tags.	No tags
kms_key_id	string	The AWS KMS key ID to be used for encrypting the stream. For more information, see Using Server-Side Encryption with Kinesis Video Streams.	The default KMS key (aws/kinesis-video.)
streaming_type	STREAMING_TYPE enumeration	The only supported value is STREAMING_TYPE_REAL-TIME.	

Field	Data Type	Description	Default Value
content_type	string	The content format of the stream. The Kinesis Video Streams console can play back content in the video/h264 format.	video/h264
max_latency	duration<uint64_t, milli>	The maximum latency in milliseconds for the stream. The stream latency pressure callback (if specified) is called when the buffer duration exceeds this amount of time. Specifying 0 indicates that no stream latency pressure callback will be called.	milliseconds::zero()
fragment_duration	duration<uint64_t>	The fragment duration that you want, in seconds. This value is used in combination with the key_frame_fragmentation value. If this value is false, Kinesis Video Streams generates fragments on a key frame after this duration elapses. For example, an Advanced Audio Coding (AAC) audio stream has each frame as a key frame. Specifying key_frame_fragmentation = false causes fragmentation to happen on a key frame after this duration expires, resulting in 2-second fragments.	2

Field	Data Type	Description	Default Value
timecode_scale	duration<uint64_t, milli>	The MKV timecode scale in milliseconds, which specifies the granularity of the timecodes for the frames within the MKV cluster. The MKV frame timecode is always relative to the start of the cluster. MKV uses a signed 16-bit value (0-32767) to represent the timecode within the cluster (fragment). Therefore, you should ensure that the frame timecode can be represented with the given timecode scale. The default timecode scale value of 1 ms ensures that the largest frame that can be represented is 32767 ms ~= 32 seconds. This is over the maximum fragment duration that is specified in Kinesis Video Streams Limits, which is 10 seconds.	1
key_frame_fragmentation	bool	Whether to produce fragments on a key frame. If true, the SDK produces a start of the fragment every time there is a key frame. If false, Kinesis Video Streams waits for at least fragment_duration and produces a new fragment on the key frame following it.	true

Field	Data Type	Description	Default Value
frame_timecodes	bool	Whether to use frame timecodes or generate time stamps using the current time callback. Many encoders don't produce time stamps with the frames. So specifying false for this parameter ensures that the frames are timestamped as they are put into Kinesis Video Streams.	true
absolute_fragment_times	bool	Kinesis Video Streams uses MKV as its underlying packaging mechanism. The MKV specification is strict about frame timecodes being relative to the beginning of the cluster (fragment). However, the cluster timecodes can be either absolute or relative to the starting time for the stream. If the time stamps are relative, the PutMedia service API call uses the optional stream start time stamp and adjust the cluster time stamps. The service always stores the fragments with their absolute time stamps.	true
fragment_acks	bool	Whether to receive application level fragment ACKs (acknowledgements) or not.	true, meaning that the SDK will receive the ACKs and act accordingly.
restart_on_error	bool	Whether to restart on specific errors.	true, meaning that the SDK tries to restart the streaming if any errors occur.

Field	Data Type	Description	Default Value
recalculate_metrics	bool	Whether to recalculate the metrics. Each call to retrieve the metrics can recalculate those to get the latest "running" value, which might create a small CPU impact. You might need to set this to false on extremely low-power/footprint devices to spare the CPU cycles. Otherwise, it's not advised to use false for this value.	true

Field	Data Type	Description	Default Value
nal_adaptation_flags	uint32_t	Specifies the Network Abstraction Layer unit (NALU) adaptation flags. If the bitstream is H.264 encoded, it can then be processed as raw or packaged in NALUs. Those are either in the Annex-B or AVCC format. Most of the elementary stream producers/consumers (read encoders/decoders) use the Annex-B format because it has some advantages, such as error recovery. Higher-level systems use the AVCC format, which is the default format for MPEG, HLS, DASH, and so on. The console playback uses the browser's MSE (media source extensions) to decode and play back the stream that uses the AVCC format. For H.264 (and for M-JPEG and H.265), the SDK provides adaptation capabilities. Many elementary streams are in the following format. In this example, `Ab` is the Annex-B start code (001 or 0001). Ab(Sps)Ab(Pps)Ab(I-frame)Ab(P/B-frame) Ab(P/B-frame).... Ab(Sps)Ab(Pps)Ab(I-frame)Ab(P/B-frame) Ab(P/B-frame) In the case of H.264, the codec private data (CPD) is in the SPS (sequence parameter set) and PPS (picture parameter set) parameters, and it can be adapted to the AVCC format. Unless the media pipeline gives the CPD separately, the application can	The default is to adapt Annex-B format to AVCC format for both the frame data and for the codec private data.

Field	Data Type	Description	Default Value
frame_rate	uint32_t	The expected frame rate. This value is used to better calculate buffering needs.	25
avg_bandwidth_bps	uint32_t	The expected average bandwidth for the stream. This value is used to better calculate buffering needs.	4 * 1024 * 1024
buffer_duration	duration<uint64_t>	The stream buffer duration, in seconds. The SDK keeps the frames in the content store for up to the buffer_duration, after which the older frames are dropped as the window moves forward. If the frame that is being dropped has not been sent to the backend, the dropped frame callback is called. If the current buffer duration is greater than max_latency, then the stream latency pressure callback is called. The buffer is trimmed to the next fragment start when the fragment persisted ACK is received. This indicates that the content has been durably persisted in the cloud, so storing the content on the local device is no longer needed.	120

Field	Data Type	Description	Default Value
replay_duration	duration<uint64_t>	The duration to roll the current reader backward to replay during an error if restarting is enabled, in seconds. The rollback stops at the buffer start (in case it has just started streaming or the persisted ACK has come along). The rollback tries to land on a key frame that indicates a fragment start. If the error that is causing the restart is not indicative of a dead host (that is, the host is still alive and contains the frame data in its internal buffers), the rollback stops at the last received ACK frame. It then rolls forward to the next key frame, because the entire fragment is already stored in the host memory.	40
connection_staleness	duration<uint64_t>	The time, in seconds, after which the stream staleness callback is called if the SDK does not receive the buffering ACK. It indicates that the frames are being sent from the device, but the backend is not acknowledging them. This condition indicates a severed connection at the intermediate hop or at the load balancer.	30
codec_id	string	The codec ID for the MKV track.	V_MPEG4/ISO/AVC
track_name	string	The MKV track name.	kinesis_video

Field	Data Type	Description	Default Value
codecPrivateData	unsigned char*	The codec private data (CPD) buffer. If the media pipeline has the information about the CPD before the stream starts, it can be set in StreamDefinition.codecPrivateData. The bits are copied, and the buffer can be reused or freed after the call to create the stream. However, if the data is not available when the stream is created, it can be set in one of the overloads of the KinesisVideoStream.start(cp function.	null
codecPrivateDataSize	uint32_t	The codec private data buffer size.	0

ClientMetrics

The **ClientMetrics** object is filled by calling `getKinesisVideoMetrics`.

Member Fields

Field	Data Type	Description
version	UINT32	The version of the structure, defined in the CLIENT_MET-RICS_CURRENT_VER-SION macro.
contentStoreSize	UINT64	The overall content store size in bytes. This is the value specified in DeviceInfo.StorageInfo.storageSize.
contentStoreAvailableSize	UINT64	Currently available storage size in bytes.
contentStoreAllocatedSize	UINT64	Currently allocated size. The allocated plus the available sizes should be slightly smaller than the overall storage size, due to the internal bookkeeping and the implementation of the content store.

Field	Data Type	Description
totalContentViewsSize	UINT64	The size of the memory allocated for all content views for all streams. This is not counted against the storage size. This memory is allocated using the MEMALLOC macro, which can be overwritten to provide a custom allocator.
totalFrameRate	UINT64	The total observed frame rate across all the streams.
totalTransferRate	UINT64	The total observed stream rate in bytes per second across all the streams.

StreamMetrics

The **StreamMetrics** object is filled by calling `getKinesisVideoMetrics`.

Member Fields

Field	Data Type	Description
version	UINT32	The version of the structure, defined in the STREAM_METRICS_CURRENT_VERSION macro.
currentViewDuration	UINT64	The duration of the accumulated frames. In the fast networking case, this duration is either 0 or the frame duration (as the frame is being transmitted). If the duration becomes longer than the max_latency specified in the StreamDefinition, the stream latency callback is called if it is specified. The duration is specified in 100 ns units, which is the default time unit for the PIC layer.

Field	Data Type	Description
overallViewDuration	UINT64	The overall view duration. If the stream is configured with no ACKs or persistence, this value grows as the frames are put into the Kinesis video stream and becomes equal to the buffer_duration in the StreamDefinition. When ACKs are enabled and the persisted ACK is received, the buffer is trimmed to the next key frame, because the ACK time stamp indicates the beginning of the entire fragment. The duration is specified in 100-ns units, which is the default time unit for the PIC layer.
currentViewSize	UINT64	The size in bytes of the current buffer.
overallViewSize	UINT64	The overall view size in bytes.
currentFrameRate	UINT64	The observed frame rate for the current stream.
currentTransferRate	UINT64	The observed transfer rate in bytes per second for the current stream.

Producer SDK Callbacks

The classes and methods in the Amazon Kinesis Video Streams Producer SDK do not maintain their own processes. Instead, they use the incoming function calls and events to schedule callbacks to communicate with the application.

There are two callback patterns that the application can use to interact with the SDK:

- `CallbackProvider`: This object exposes every callback from the platform-independent code (PIC) component to the application. This pattern allows full functionality, but it also means that the implementation must handle all of the public API methods and signatures in the C++ layer.
- StreamCallbackProvider and ClientCallbackProvider: These objects expose the stream-specific and client-specific callbacks, and the C++ layer of the SDK exposes the rest of the callbacks. This is the preferred callback pattern for interacting with the Producer SDK.

The following diagram illustrates the object model of the callback objects:

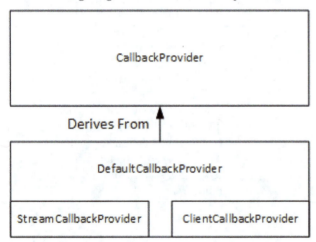

In the preceding diagram, `DefaultCallbackProvider` derives from `CallbackProvider` (which exposes all of the callbacks in the PIC) and contains `StreamCallbackProvider` and `ClientCallbackProvider`.

Topics

- ClientCallbackProvider
- StreamCallbackProvider
- ClientCallbacks Structure

ClientCallbackProvider

The `ClientCallbackProvider` object exposes client-level callback functions. The details of the functions are described in the ClientCallbacks section.

Callback methods:

- `getClientReadyCallback`: Reports a ready state for the client.
- `getStorageOverflowPressureCallback`: Reports storage overflow or pressure. This callback is called when the storage utilization exceeds the `STORAGE_PRESSURE_NOTIFICATION_THRESHOLD` value, which is 5 percent of the overall storage size. For more information, see StorageInfo.

For the source code for `ClientCallbackProvider`, see Include.h.

StreamCallbackProvider

The `StreamCallbackProvider` object exposes stream-level callback functions.

Callback methods:

- `getDroppedFragmentReportCallback`: Reports a dropped fragment.
- `getDroppedFrameReportCallback`: Reports a dropped frame.
- `getFragmentAckReceivedCallback`: Reports that a fragment ACK is received for the stream.
- `getStreamClosedCallback`: Reports a stream closed condition.
- `getStreamConnectionStaleCallback`: Reports a stale connection condition. In this condition, the producer is sending data to the service but is not receiving acknowledgements.
- `getStreamDataAvailableCallback`: Reports that data is available in the stream.
- `getStreamErrorReportCallback`: Reports a stream error condition.
- `getStreamLatencyPressureCallback`: Reports a stream latency condition, which is when the accumulated buffer size is larger than the `max_latency` value. For more information, see StreamDefinition/ StreamInfo.
- `getStreamReadyCallback`: Reports a stream ready condition.
- `getStreamUnderflowReportCallback`: Reports a stream underflow condition. This function is not currently used and is reserved for future use.

For the source code for **StreamCallbackProvider**, see StreamCallbackProvider.h.

ClientCallbacks Structure

The `ClientCallbacks` structure contains the callback function entry points that the PIC calls when specific events occur. The structure also contains version information in the `CALLBACKS_CURRENT_VERSION` field, and a `customData` field for user-defined data that is returned with the individual callback functions.

The client application can use a `this` pointer for the `custom_data` field to map member functions to the static `ClientCallback` functions at runtime, as shown in the following code example:

```
1 STATUS TestStreamCallbackProvider::streamClosedHandler(UINT64 custom_data, STREAM_HANDLE
    stream_handle, UINT64 stream_upload_handle) {
2   LOG_INFO("Reporting stream stopped.");
3
4 TestStreamCallbackProvider* streamCallbackProvider = reinterpret_cast<TestStreamCallbackProvider
    *> (custom_data);
5 streamCallbackProvider->streamClosedHandler(...);
```

Events

Function	Description	Type
CreateDeviceFunc	Not currently implemented on the backend. This call fails when called from Java or C++. Other clients perform platform-specific initialization.	Backend API
CreateStreamFunc	Called when the stream is created.	Backend API
DescribeStreamFunc	Called when DescribeStream is called.	Backend API
GetStreamingEndpointFunc	Called when GetStreamingEndpoint is called.	Backend API
GetStreamingTokenFunc	Called when GetStreamingToken is called.	Backend API

Function	Description	Type
PutStreamFunc	Called when PutStream is called.	Backend API
TagResourceFunc	Called when TagResource is called.	Backend API
CreateMutexFunc	Creates a synchronization mutex.	Synchronization
FreeMutexFunc	Frees the mutex.	Synchronization
LockMutexFunc	Locks the synchronization mutex.	Synchronization
TryLockMutexFunc	Tries to lock the mutex. Not currently implemented.	Synchronization
UnlockMutexFunc	Unlocks the mutex.	Synchronization
ClientReadyFunc	Called when the client enters a ready state.	Notification
DroppedFrameReportFunc	Reports when a frame is dropped.	Notification
DroppedFragmentReportFunc	Reports when a fragment is dropped. This function is not currently used and is reserved for future use.	Notification
FragmentAckReceivedFunc	Called when a fragment ACK (buffering, received, persisted, and error) is received.	Notification
StorageOverflowPressureFunc	Called when the storage utilization exceeds the STORAGE_PRESSURE_NOTIFICATION_THRESHOLD value, which is defined as 5 percent of the overall storage size.	Notification
StreamClosedFunc	Called when the last bits of the remaining frames are streamed.	Notification
StreamConnectionStaleFunc	Called when the stream enters a stale connection state. In this condition, the producer is sending data to the service but is not receiving acknowledgements.	Notification
StreamDataAvailableFunc	Called when stream data is available.	Notification
StreamErrorReportFunc	Called when a stream error occurs. The PIC automatically closes the stream under this condition.	Notification

Function	Description	Type
StreamLatencyPressureFunc	Called when the stream enters a latency condition, which is when the accumulated buffer size is larger than the max_latency value. For more information, see StreamDefinition/ StreamInfo.	Notification
StreamReadyFunc	Called when the stream enters the ready state.	Notification
StreamUnderflowReportFunc	This function is not currently used and is reserved for future use.	Notification
DeviceCertToTokenFunc	Returns the connection certificate as a token.	Platform integration
GetCurrentTimeFunc	Returns the current time.	Platform integration
GetDeviceCertificateFunc	Returns the device certificate. This function is not currently used and is reserved for future use.	Platform integration
GetDeviceFingerprintFunc	Returns the device fingerprint. This function is not currently used and is reserved for future use.	Platform integration
GetRandomNumberFunc	Returns a random number between 0 and RAND_MAX.	Platform integration
GetSecurityTokenFunc	Returns the security token that is passed to the functions that communicate with the backend API. The implementation can specify the serialized AccessKeyId, SecretKeyId, and the session token.	Platform integration
LogPrintFunc	Logs a line of text with the tag and the log level. For more information, see PlatformUtils.h.	Platform integration

For the platform integration functions in the preceding table, the last parameter is a `ServiceCallContext` structure, which has the following fields:

- `version`: The version of the struct.
- `callAfter`: An absolute time after which to call the function.
- `timeout`: The timeout of the operation in 100 nanosecond units.
- `customData`: A user-defined value to be passed back to the client.
- `pAuthInfo`: The credentials for the call. For more information, see the following (`__AuthInfo`) structure.

The authorization information is provided using the `__AuthInfo` structure, which can be either serialized credentials or a provider-specific authentication token. This structure has the following fields:

- `version`: The version of the `__AuthInfo` structure.
- `type`: An `AUTH_INFO_TYPE` value defining the type of the credential (certificate or security token).
- `data`: A byte array containing the authentication information.

- **size**: The size of the **data** parameter.
- **expiration**: The expiration of the credentials in 100 nanosecond units.

Kinesis Video Stream Parser Library

The Kinesis Video Stream Parser Library is an easy-to-use set of tools you can use in Java applications to consume the MKV data in a Kinesis video stream.

The library includes the following tools:

- StreamingMkvReader: This class reads specified MKV elements from a video stream.
- FragmentMetadataVisitor: This class retrieves metadata for fragments (media elements) and tracks (individual data streams containing media information, such as audio or subtitles).
- OutputSegmentMerger: This class merges consecutive fragments or chunks in a video stream.
- KinesisVideoExample: This is a sample application that shows how to use the Kinesis Video Stream Parser Library.

The library also includes tests that show how the tools are used.

Procedure: Using the Kinesis Video Stream Parser Library

This procedure includes the following steps:

- Step 1: Download and Configure the Code
- Step 2: Write and Examine the Code
- Step 3: Run and Verify the Code

Prerequisites

You must have the following to examine and use the Kinesis Video Stream Parser Library:

- An Amazon Web Services (AWS) account. If you don't already have an AWS account, do the following:

  - Open https://aws.amazon.com/, and then choose **Create an AWS Account**. **Note**
    This might be unavailable in your browser if you previously signed in to the AWS Management Console. In that case, choose **Sign In to the Console**, and then choose **Create a new AWS account**.

  - Follow the online instructions.

    Part of the sign-up procedure involves receiving a phone call and entering a PIN using the phone keypad.

  Note your AWS account ID because you need it for configuring programmatic access to Kinesis video streams.

- A Java integrated development environment (IDE), such as Eclipse Java Neon or JetBrains IntelliJ Idea.

Step 1: Download and Configure the Code

In this section, you download the Java library and test code and import the project into your Java IDE.

For prerequisites and other details about this procedure, see Kinesis Video Stream Parser Library.

1. Create a directory and clone the library source code from the GitHub repository.

```
1 $ git clone https://github.com/aws/amazon-kinesis-video-streams-parser-library
```

2. Open the Java IDE that you are using (for example, Eclipse or IntelliJ IDEA) and import the Apache Maven project that you downloaded:

   - **In Eclipse:** Choose **File**, **Import**, **Maven**, **Existing Maven Projects**, and navigate to the `kinesis-video-streams-parser-lib` folder.
   - **In IntelliJ Idea: ** Choose **Import**. Navigate to the **pom.xml** file in the root of the downloaded package.

   For more information, see the related IDE documentation.

Next Step

Step 2: Write and Examine the Code

Amazon Kinesis Video Streams Examples

The following code examples demonstrate how to work with the Kinesis Video Streams API:

- GStreamer Plugin: Shows how to build the Kinesis Video Streams Producer SDK to use as a GStreamer destination.
- Example: Sending Data to Kinesis Video Streams Using the PutMedia API: Send data that is already in a container format (MKV) using the PutMedia API.
- Example: Streaming from an RTSP Source: Sample application that runs in a Docker container and streams video from an RTSP source.
- Example: Using GStreamer with Kinesis Video Streams: Send video data to Kinesis Video Streams using the GStreamer open source multimedia framework.
- Example: Parsing and Rendering Kinesis Video Streams Fragments: Parse and render Kinesis video stream fragments using JCodec and JFrame.
- KinesisVideoExample: Parse and log video fragments using the Kinesis Video Streams Parser Library.

Prerequisites

- In the sample code, you provide credentials by specifying a profile that you set in your AWS credentials profile file, or by providing credentials in the Java system properties of your integrated development environment (IDE). So if you haven't already done so, first set up your credentials. For more information, see Set up AWS Credentials and Region for Development.
- We recommend that you use a Java IDE to view and run the code, such as one of the following:
    - Eclipse Java Neon
    - JetBrains IntelliJ IDEA

Example: Kinesis Video Streams Producer SDK GStreamer Plugin

This topic shows how to build the Amazon Kinesis Video Streams Producer SDK to use as a GStreamer plugin.

Topics

- Download, Build, and Configure the GStreamer Element
- Run the GStreamer Element
- Example GStreamer Launch Commands
- Run the GStreamer Element in a Docker Container
- GStreamer Element Parameter Reference

GStreamer is a popular media framework used by a multitude of cameras and video sources to create custom media pipelines by combining modular plugins. The Kinesis Video Streams GStreamer plugin greatly simplifies the integration of your existing GStreamer media pipeline with Kinesis Video Streams. After integrating GStreamer, you can get started with streaming video from a webcam or RTSP (Real Time Streaming Protocol) camera to Kinesis Video Streams for real-time or later playback, storage, and further analysis.

The GStreamer plugin automatically manages the transfer of your video stream to Kinesis Video Streams by encapsulating the functionality provided by the Kinesis Video Streams Producer SDK in a GStreamer sink element, `kvssink`. The GStreamer framework provides a standard managed environment for constructing media flow from a device such as a camera or other video source for further processing, rendering, or storage.

The GStreamer pipeline typically consists of the link between a source (video camera) and the sink element (either a player to render the video, or storage for offline retrieval). In this example, you use the Producer SDK element as a *sink*, or media destination, for your video source (webcam or IP camera). The plugin element that encapsulates the SDK then manages sending the video stream to Kinesis Video Streams.

This topic shows how to construct a GStreamer media pipeline capable of streaming video from a video source, such as a web camera or RTSP stream, typically connected through intermediate encoding stages (using H.264 encoding) to Kinesis Video Streams. When your video stream is available as a Kinesis video stream, you can use the Kinesis Video Stream Parser Library for further processing, playback, storage, or analysis of your video stream.

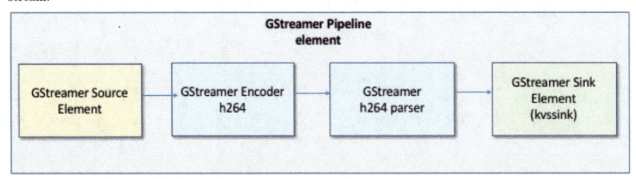

Download, Build, and Configure the GStreamer Element

The GStreamer Plugin example is included with the Kinesis Video Streams C++ Producer SDK. For information about SDK prerequisites and downloading, see Step 1: Download and Configure the C++ Producer Library Code.

To build the Producer SDK GStreamer sink as a dynamic library on macOS, Ubuntu, or Raspberry Pi, execute the following command in the `kinesis-video-native-build` directory:

```
1  ./gstreamer-plugin-install-script
```

After the sink is built, you can execute `gst-launch-1.0` from the following directory:

```
1 <YourSdkFolderPath>/kinesis-video-native-build/downloads/local/bin
```

You can either run `gst-launch-1.0` from this directory, or add it to the `PATH` environment variable:

```
1 $ export PATH=<YourSdkFolderPath>/kinesis-video-native-build/downloads/local/bin:$PATH
```

Add the library directory to your path so that the GStreamer plugin can be found:

```
1 export GST_PLUGIN_PATH=<YourSdkFolderPath>/kinesis-video-native-build/downloads/local/lib:
    $GST_PLUGIN_PATH
```

Set the library path for the SDK:

```
1 export LD_LIBRARY_PATH=<YourSdkFolderPath>/kinesis-video-native-build/downloads/local/lib
```

Run the GStreamer Element

To run GStreamer with the Kinesis Video Streams Producer SDK element as a sink, execute the `gst-launch-1.0` command. Use settings that are appropriate for the GStreamer plugin to use—for example, v412src for v412 devices on Linux systems, or rtspsrc for RTSP devices. Specify `kvssink` as the sink (final destination of the pipeline) to send video to the Producer SDK.

The `kvssink` element has the following required parameters:

- `stream-name`: The name of the destination Kinesis video stream.
- `storage-size`: The storage size of the device in kilobytes. For information about configuring device storage, see StorageInfo.
- `access-key`: The AWS access key that is used to access Kinesis Video Streams. You must provide either this parameter or `credential-path`.
- `secret-key`: The AWS secret key that is used to access Kinesis Video Streams. You must provide either this parameter or `credential-path`.
- `credential-path`: A path to a file containing your credentials for accessing Kinesis Video Streams. For example credential files, see Sample Static Credential and Sample Rotating Credential. For more information on rotating credentials, see Managing Access Keys for IAM Users. You must provide either this parameter or `access-key` and `secret-key`.

For information about `kvssink` optional parameters, see GStreamer Element Parameter Reference.

For the latest information about GStreamer plugins and parameters, see GStreamer Plugins, or execute the following command to list options:

```
1 gst-inspect-1.0 kvssink
```

Example GStreamer Launch Commands

These examples demonstrate how to use a GStreamer plugin to stream video from different types of devices.

Example 1: Stream Video from an RTSP Camera on Ubuntu

The following command creates a GStreamer pipeline on Ubuntu that streams from a network RTSP camera, using the rtspsrc GStreamer plugin:

```
1 $ gst-launch-1.0 rtspsrc location"=rtsp://"YourCameraRtspUrl short-header=TRUE ! rtph264depay !
    video/x-h264, format=avc,alignment=au ! kvssink stream-name"="YourStreamName storage-size
    =512 access-key="YourAccessKey" secret-key="YourSecretKey"
```

Example 2: Encode and Stream Video from a USB Camera on Ubuntu

The following command creates a GStreamer pipeline on Ubuntu that encodes the stream from a USB camera in H.264 format, and streams it to Kinesis Video Streams. This example uses the v4l2src GStreamer plugin.

```
1 $ gst-launch-1.0 v4l2src do-timestamp=TRUE device=/dev/video0 ! videoconvert ! video/x-raw,
    format=I420,width=640,height=480,framerate=30/1 ! x264enc  bframes=0 key-int-max=45 bitrate
    =500 ! video/x-h264,stream-format=avc,alignment=au,profile=baseline ! kvssink stream-name="
    YourStreamName" storage-size=512 access-key="YourAccessKey" secret-key="YourSecretKey"
```

Example 3: Stream Pre-Encoded Video from a USB Camera on Ubuntu

The following command creates a GStreamer pipeline on Ubuntu that streams video that the camera has already encoded in H.264 format to Kinesis Video Streams. This example uses the v4l2src GStreamer plugin.

```
1 $ gst-launch-1.0 v4l2src do-timestamp=TRUE device=/dev/video0 ! h264parse ! video/x-h264,stream-
    format=avc,alignment=au ! kvssink stream-name="plugin" storage-size=512 access-key="
    YourAccessKey" secret-key="YourSecretKey"
```

Example 4: Stream Video from a Camera on macOS

The following command creates a GStreamer pipeline on macOS that streams video to Kinesis Video Streams. This example uses the autovideosrc GStreamer plugin.

```
1 $ gst-launch-1.0 autovideosrc ! videoconvert ! video/x-raw,format=I420,width=640,height=480,
    framerate=30/1 ! vtenc_h264_hw allow-frame-reordering=FALSE realtime=TRUE max-keyframe-
    interval=45 bitrate=500 ! h264parse ! video/x-h264,stream-format=avc,alignment=au,width=640,
    height=480,framerate=30/1,profile=baseline ! kvssink stream-name="YourStreamName" storage-
    size=512 access-key="YourAccessKey" secret-key="YourSecretKey"
```

Example 5: Stream Video from a Camera on Raspberry Pi

The following command creates a GStreamer pipeline on Raspberry Pi that streams video to Kinesis Video Streams. This example uses the v4l2src GStreamer plugin.

```
1 $ gst-launch-1.0 v4l2src do-timestamp=TRUE device=/dev/video0 ! videoconvert ! video/x-raw,
    format=I420,width=640,height=480,framerate=30/1 ! omxh264enc control-rate=1 target-bitrate
    =5120000 periodicity-idr=45 inline-header=FALSE ! h264parse ! video/x-h264,stream-format=avc
    ,alignment=au,width=640,height=480,framerate=30/1,profile=baseline ! kvssink stream-name="
    YourStreamName" frame-timestamp=dts-only access-key="YourAccessKey" secret-key="
    YourSecretKey"
```

Run the GStreamer Element in a Docker Container

Docker is a platform for developing, deploying, and running applications using containers. Using Docker to create the GStreamer pipeline standardizes the operating environment for Kinesis Video Streams, which greatly simplifies building and executing the application.

To install and configure Docker, see the following:

- Docker download instructions
- Getting started with Docker

114

After installing Docker, you can download the Kinesis Video Streams C++ Producer SDK (and GStreamer plugin) from Amazon Elastic Container Registry using the `docker pull` command.

To run GStreamer with the Kinesis Video Streams Producer SDK element as a sink in a Docker container, do the following:

Topics

- Authenticate your Docker Client
- Download the Docker image for Ubuntu, macOS, or Raspberry Pi
- Run the Docker Image

Authenticate your Docker Client

Authenticate your Docker client to the Amazon ECR registry that you intend to pull your image from. You must get authentication tokens for each registry used, and the tokens are valid for 12 hours. For more information, see Registry Authentication in the *Amazon Elastic Container Registry User Guide.*

Example : Authenticate with Amazon ECR

```
1 aws ecr get-login --no-include-email --region us-west-2 --registry-ids 546150905175
```

The preceding command produces output similar to the following:

```
1 docker login -u AWS -p <Password>   https://YourAccountId.dkr.ecr.us-west-2.amazonaws.com
```

The resulting output is a Docker login command that you use to authenticate your Docker client to your Amazon ECR registry.

Download the Docker image for Ubuntu, macOS, or Raspberry Pi

Download the Docker image to your Docker environment using one the following commands, depending on your operating system:

Download the Docker image for Ubuntu

```
1 sudo docker pull 546150905175.dkr.ecr.us-west-2.amazonaws.com/kinesis-video-producer-sdk-cpp-
    amazon-linux:latest
```

Download the Docker image for macOS

```
1 sudo docker pull 546150905175.dkr.ecr.us-west-2.amazonaws.com/kinesis-video-producer-sdk-cpp-
    amazon-linux:latest
```

Download the Docker image for Raspberry Pi

```
1 sudo docker pull 546150905175.dkr.ecr.us-west-2.amazonaws.com/kinesis-video-producer-sdk-cpp-
    raspberry-pi:latest
```

To verify that the image was successfully added, use the following command:

```
1 docker images
```

Run the Docker Image

Use one of the following commands to run the Docker image, depending on your operating system:

Run the Docker Image on Ubuntu

```
1 sudo docker run -it --network="host" --device=/dev/video0 546150905175
2 .dkr.ecr.us-west-2.amazonaws.com/kinesis-video-producer-sdk-cpp-amazon-linux /bin/bash
```

Run the Docker Image on macOS

```
1 sudo docker run -it --network="host" --device=/dev/video0 --device=/dev/video1 546150905175
2 .dkr.ecr.us-west-2.amazonaws.com/kinesis-video-producer-sdk-cpp-amazon-linux /bin/bash
```

Run the Docker Image on Raspberry Pi

```
1 sudo docker run -it --device=/dev/video0 --device=/dev/vchiq -v /opt/vc:/opt/vc 546150905175
2 .dkr.ecr.us-west-2.amazonaws.com/kinesis-video-producer-sdk-cpp-raspberry-pi /bin/bash
```

Docker launches the container, and presents you with a command prompt for executing commands within the container.

In the container, set the environment variables using the following command:

```
1 export LD_LIBRARY_PATH=/opt/awssdk/amazon-kinesis-video-streams-producer-sdk-cpp/kinesis-video-
      native-build/downloads/local/lib:$LD_LIBRARY_PATH
2 export PATH=/opt/awssdk/amazon-kinesis-video-streams-producer-sdk-cpp/kinesis-video-native-build
      /downloads/local/bin:$PATH
3 export GST_PLUGIN_PATH=/opt/awssdk/amazon-kinesis-video-streams-producer-sdk-cpp/kinesis-video-
      native-build/downloads/local/lib:$GST_PLUGIN_PATH
```

Start streaming from the camera using the gst-launch-1.0 command that is appropriate for your device.

For examples of using the gst-launch-1.0 command to connect to a local web camera or a network RTSP camera, see Launch Commands.

GStreamer Element Parameter Reference

To send video to the Amazon Kinesis Video Streams Producer SDK, you specify `kvssink` as the *sink*, or final destination of the pipeline. This reference provides information about `kvssink` required and optional parameters. For more information, see Example: Kinesis Video Streams Producer SDK GStreamer Plugin.

The `kvssink` element has the following required parameters:

- `stream-name`: The name of the destination Kinesis video stream.
- `storage-size`: The storage size of the device in kilobytes. For information about configuring device storage, see StorageInfo.
- `access-key`: The AWS access key that is used to access Kinesis Video Streams. You must provide either this parameter or `credential-path`.
- `secret-key`: The AWS secret key that is used to access Kinesis Video Streams. You must provide either this parameter or `credential-path`.
- `credential-path`: A path to a file containing your credentials for accessing Kinesis Video Streams. For example credential files, see Sample Static Credential and Sample Rotating Credential. You must provide either this parameter or `access-key` and `secret-key`.

The `kvssink` element has the following optional parameters. For more information about these parameters, see Kinesis Video Stream Structures.

Parameter	Description	Unit/ Type	Default
retention-period	The length of time the stream is preserved.	Hours	2
streaming-type	The streaming type. Valid values include: [See the AWS documentation website for more details]	Enum GstKvsSinkStreaming-Type	0: real time
content-type	The content type of the stream.	String	"video/h264"
max-latency	The maximum latency for the stream.	Seconds	60
fragment-duration	The fragment duration that you want.	Milliseconds	2000
timecode-scale	The MKV timecode scale.	Milliseconds	1
key-frame-fragmentation	Whether to produce fragments on a key frame.	Boolean	true
frame-timecodes	Whether to use frame timecodes or generate time stamps using the current time callback.	Boolean	true
absolute-fragment-times	Whether to use absolute fragment times.	Boolean	true
fragment-acks	Whether to use fragment ACKs.	Boolean	true
restart-on-error	Whether to restart when an error occurs.	Boolean	true
recalculate-metrics	Whether to recalculate the metrics.	Boolean	true

Parameter	Description	Unit/ Type	Default
framerate	The expected frame rate.	Frames per second	25
avg-bandwidth-bps	The expected average bandwidth for the stream.	Bytes per second	4194304
buffer-duration	The stream buffer duration.	Seconds	180
replay-duration	The duration to roll the current reader backward to replay during an error if restarting is enabled.	Seconds	40
connection-staleness	The time after which the stream staleness callback is called.	Seconds	60
codec-id	The codec ID of the stream.	String	"V_MPEG4/ISO/AVC"
track-name	The MKV track name.	String	"kinesis_video"
rotation-period	The key rotation period. For more information, see Rotating Customer Master Keys.	Seconds	2400
log-config	The log configuration path.	String	"./kvs_log_configuration"
frame-timestamp	[See the AWS documentation website for more details]	Enum GstKvsSink-FrameTimestamp-Type	default-timestamp

Example: Sending Data to Kinesis Video Streams Using the Put-Media API

This example demonstrates how to use the PutMedia API. It shows how to send data that is already in a container format (MKV). If your data needs to be assembled into a container format before sending (for example, if you are assembling camera video data into frames), see Kinesis Video Streams Producer Libraries.

Note
The `PutMedia` operation is available only in the C++ and Java SDKs, due to the full-duplex management of connections, data flow, and acknowledgements. It is not supported in other languages.

Topics

- Step 1: Download and Configure the Code
- Step 2: Write and Examine the Code
- Step 3: Run and Verify the Code

Step 1: Download and Configure the Code

In this section, you download the Java example code, import the project into your Java IDE, configure the library locations, and configure the code to use your AWS credentials.

1. Create a directory and clone the example source code from the GitHub repository. The `PutMedia` example is part of the Java Producer Library.

```
1 $ git clone https://github.com/awslabs/amazon-kinesis-video-streams-producer-sdk-java
```

2. Open the Java IDE that you are using (for example, Eclipse or IntelliJ IDEA), and import the Apache Maven project that you downloaded:

   - **In Eclipse:** Choose **File**, **Import**, **Maven**, **Existing Maven Projects**, and navigate to the root of the downloaded package. Select the `pom.xml` file.
   - **In IntelliJ Idea: ** Choose **Import**. Navigate to the `pom.xml` file in the root of the downloaded package.

   For more information, see the related IDE documentation.

3. Update the project so that the IDE can find the libraries that you imported.

   - For IntelliJ IDEA, do the following:

     1. Open the context (right-click) menu for the project's **lib** directory, and choose **Add as library**.

     2. Choose **File**, **Project Structure**.

     3. Under **Project Settings**, choose **Modules**.

     4. In the **Sources** tab, set **Language Level** to **7** or higher.

   - For Eclipse, do the following:

     1. Open the context (right-click) menu for the project, and choose **Properties**, **Java Build Path**, **Source**. Then do the following:

        1. On the **Source** tab, double-click **Native library location**.

        2. In the **Native Library Folder Configuration** wizard, choose **Workspace**.

        3. In the **Native Library Folder** selection, choose the **lib** directory in the project.

     2. Open the context (right-click) menu for the project, and choose **Properties**. Then do the following:

119

1. On the **Libraries** tab, choose **Add Jars**.

2. In the **JAR selection** wizard, choose all .jars in the project's `lib` directory.

Step 2: Write and Examine the Code

The `PutMedia` API example (`PutMediaDemo`) shows the following coding pattern:

Topics

- Create the PutMediaClient
- Stream Media and Pause the Thread

The code examples in this section are from the `PutMediaDemo` class.

Create the PutMediaClient

Creating the `PutMediaClient` object takes the following parameters:

- The URI for the `PutMedia` endpoint.

- An `InputStream` pointing to the MKV file to stream.

- The stream name. This example uses the stream that was created in the Using the Java Producer Library (**my-stream**). To use a different stream, change the following parameter:

```
1 private static final String STREAM_NAME="my-stream";
```

Note

The `PutMedia` API example does not create a stream. You must create a stream either by using the test application for the Using the Java Producer Library, by using the Kinesis Video Streams console, or by using the AWS CLI.

- The current time stamp.
- The time code type. The example uses `RELATIVE`, indicating that the time stamp is relative to the start of the container.
- An `AWSKinesisVideoV4Signer` object that verifies that the received packets were sent by the authorized sender.
- The maximum upstream bandwidth in Kbps.
- An `AckConsumer` object to receive packet received acknowledgements.

The following code creates the `PutMediaClient` object:

```
1 /* actually URI to send PutMedia request */
2 final URI uri = URI.create(KINESIS_VIDEO_DATA_ENDPOINT + PUT_MEDIA_API);
3
4 /* input stream for sample MKV file */
5 final InputStream inputStream = new FileInputStream(MKV_FILE_PATH);
6
7 /* use a latch for main thread to wait for response to complete */
8 final CountDownLatch latch = new CountDownLatch(1);
9
10 /* a consumer for PutMedia ACK events */
11 final AckConsumer ackConsumer = new AckConsumer(latch);
12
13 /* client configuration used for AWS SigV4 signer */
14 final ClientConfiguration configuration = getClientConfiguration(uri);
15
16 /* PutMedia client */
```

```
17  final PutMediaClient client = PutMediaClient.builder()
18          .putMediaDestinationUri(uri)
19          .mkvStream(inputStream)
20          .streamName(STREAM_NAME)
21          .timestamp(System.currentTimeMillis())
22          .fragmentTimeCodeType("RELATIVE")
23          .signWith(getKinesisVideoSigner(configuration))
24          .upstreamKbps(MAX_BANDWIDTH_KBPS)
25          .receiveAcks(ackConsumer)
26          .build();
```

Stream Media and Pause the Thread

After the client is created, the sample starts asynchronous streaming with `putMediaInBackground`. The main thread is then paused with `latch.await` until the `AckConsumer` returns, at which point the client is closed.

```
1   /* start streaming video in a background thread */
2             client.putMediaInBackground();
3
4             /* wait for request/response to complete */
5             latch.await();
6
7             /* close the client */
8             client.close();
```

Step 3: Run and Verify the Code

To run the `PutMedia` API example, do the following:

1. Create a stream named **my-stream** in the Kinesis Video Streams console or by using the AWS CLI.

2. Change your working directory to the Java producer SDK directory:

```
1  $ cd /<YOUR_FOLDER_PATH_WHERE_SDK_IS_DOWNLOADED>/amazon-kinesis-video-streams-producer-sdk-
       java/
```

3. Compile the Java SDK and demo application:

```
1  mvn package
```

4. Create a temporary filename in the `/tmp` directory:

```
1  $ jar_files=$(mktemp)
```

5. Create a classpath string of dependencies from the local repository to a file:

```
1  $ mvn -Dmdep.outputFile=$jar_files dependency:build-classpath
```

6. Set the value of the `LD_LIBRARY_PATH` environment variable as follows:

```
1  $ export LD_LIBRARY_PATH=/<YOUR_FOLDER_PATH_WHERE_SDK_IS_DOWNLOADED>/amazon-kinesis-video-
       streams-producer-sdk-cpp/kinesis-video-native-build/downloads/local/lib:
       $LD_LIBRARY_PATH
2  $ classpath_values=$(cat $jar_files)
```

7. Run the demo from the command line as follows, providing your AWS credentials:

```
1 $ java -classpath target/kinesisvideo-java-demo-1.0-SNAPSHOT.jar:$classpath_values -Daws.
    accessKeyId=${ACCESS_KEY} -Daws.secretKey=${SECRET_KEY} -Djava.library.path=/opt/amazon
    -kinesis-video-streams-producer-sdk-cpp/kinesis-video-native-build com.amazonaws.
    kinesisvideo.demoapp.DemoAppMain
```

8. Open the Kinesis Video Streams console at https://console.aws.amazon.com/kinesisvideo/, and choose your stream on the **Manage Streams** page. The video plays in the **Video Preview** pane.

Example: Streaming from an RTSP Source

The C++ Producer Library contains a definition for a Docker container that connects to an RTSP (Real Time Streaming Protocol) network camera. Using Docker standardizes the operating environment for Kinesis Video Streams, which greatly simplifies building and executing the application.

To use the RTSP demo application, first install and build the C++ Producer Library.

The following procedure demonstrates how to set up and use the RTSP demo application.

Topics

- Prerequisites
- Build the Docker Image
- Run the RTSP Example Application

Prerequisites

To run the Kinesis Video Streams RTSP example application, you must have the following:

- **Docker:** For information about installing and using Docker, see the following links:
  - Docker download instructions
  - Getting started with Docker
- **RTSP network camera source:** For information about recommended cameras, see System Requirements.

Build the Docker Image

First, you build the Docker image that the demo application will run inside.

1. Create a new directory and copy the following files from the `docker_native_scripts` directory to the new directory:

   - `Dockerfile`
   - `start_rtsp_in_docker.sh`

2. Change to the directory that you created in the previous step.

3. Build the Docker image using the following command. This command creates the image and tags it as `rtspdockertest`.

```
1 docker build -t rtspdockertest .
```

4. Record the image ID that was returned in the previous step (for example, *54f0d65f69b2*).

Run the RTSP Example Application

Start the Kinesis Video Streams Docker container using the following command. Provide the image ID from the previous step, your AWS credentials, the URL of your RTSP network camera, and the name of the Kinesis video stream to send the data.

```
1 $ docker run -it <IMAGE_ID> <AWS_ACCESS_KEY_ID> <AWS_SECRET_ACCESS_KEY> <RTSP_URL> <STREAM_NAME>
```

To customize the application, comment or remove the `ENTRYPOINT` command in `Dockerfile`, and launch the container using the following command:

```
1 docker run -it <IMAGE_ID> bash
```

You are then prompted inside the Docker container to customize the sample application and start streaming.

Example: Using GStreamer with Kinesis Video Streams

The C++ Producer Library contains a demo application for using GStreamer, an open source multimedia framework, with Amazon Kinesis Video Streams.

The following procedure demonstrates how to set up and use the GStreamer demo. The application sends the video data to Kinesis Video Streams on the following platforms:

- A built-in camera on a macOS computer
- A USB camera on a Linux or Raspberry Pi device

Note
The GStreamer example is not currently available for Windows systems.

Prerequisites

The GStreamer example typically requires the following components, which you can install using the following commands:

- Automake: `brew install automake`
- Autoconf: `brew install autoconf automake`
- CMake: `brew install cmake`
- GStreamer: `brew install gstreamer gst-plugins-base gst-plugins-bad gst-plugins-good gst-plugins-ugly`
- GNU Bison: `brew install bison && brew link bison --force`

For a more comprehensive list of requirements, see Prerequisites in the C++ Producer SDK documentation, or the `README.md` file in the SDK itself.

Running the GStreamer Example

1. Create a directory, and then clone the example source code from the GitHub repository.

   ```
   1 $ git clone https://github.com/awslabs/amazon-kinesis-video-streams-producer-sdk-cpp
   ```

2. Run the following script in the `/kinesis-video-native-build` directory to build the C++ Producer SDK:

   ```
   1 ./install-script
   ```

   This script installs the prerequisites for the SDK and builds the binaries, including the GStreamer example. For information about building the example on Ubuntu, see the "Troubleshooting" section of the `README.md` file in the SDK.

3. After the C++ Procedure SDK is installed and configured, run the application using the following command (also in the `/kinesis-video-native-build` directory):

   ```
   1 export AWS_ACCESS_KEY_ID=AKIAIOSFODNN7EXAMPLE
   2 export AWS_SECRET_ACCESS_KEY=wJalrXUtnFEMI/K7MDENG/bPxRfiCYEXAMPLEKEY
   3 export AWS_DEFAULT_REGION=<AWS region>
   4 ./kinesis_video_gstreamer_sample_app stream_name
   ```

   Supply the following information for the application parameters:

   - **AWS_ACCESS_KEY_ID:** The access key ID for your account. See Prerequisites.
   - **AWS_SECRET_ACCESS_KEY:** The secret access key for your account. See Prerequisites.
   - **AWS_DEFAULT_REGION:** Your AWS Region, for example, `us-west-2`.

- **stream_name:** The name of the Kinesis video stream to send camera data to. The stream will be created if it doesn't exist.

4. The demo application starts. In a few seconds, you will see video data from your camera in the Kinesis Video Streams console for your stream. **Note**
   If the application fails to acquire your camera, you might see a `Failed to negotiate pipeline` error. For troubleshooting information, see the `README.md` file in the SDK.

Example: Parsing and Rendering Kinesis Video Streams Fragments

The Stream Parser Library contains a demo application named `KinesisVideoRendererExample` that demonstrates parsing and rendering Amazon Kinesis video stream fragments. The example uses JCodec to decode the H.264 encoded frames that are ingested using the Example: Using GStreamer with Kinesis Video Streams application. After the frame is decoded using JCodec, the visible image is rendered using JFrame.

This example shows how to do the following:

- Retrieve frames from a Kinesis video stream using the `GetMedia` API and render the stream for viewing.
- View the video content of streams in a custom application instead of using the Kinesis Video Streams console.

You can also use the classes in this example to view Kinesis video stream content that isn't encoded as H.264, such as a stream of JPEG files that don't require decoding before being displayed.

The following procedure demonstrates how to set up and use the Renderer demo application.

Prerequisites

To examine and use the Renderer example library, you must have the following:

- An Amazon Web Services (AWS) account. If you don't already have an AWS account, see Getting Started with Kinesis Video Streams
- A Java integrated development environment (IDE), such as Eclipse Java Neon or JetBrains IntelliJ Idea.

Running the Renderer Example

1. Create a directory, and then clone the example source code from the GitHub repository.

```
1 $ git clone https://github.com/aws/amazon-kinesis-video-streams-parser-library
```

2. Open the Java IDE that you are using (for example, Eclipse or IntelliJ IDEA) and import the Apache Maven project that you downloaded:

   - **In Eclipse:** Choose **File**, **Import**, **Maven**, **Existing Maven Projects**. Navigate to the `kinesis-video-streams-parser-lib` directory.
   - **In IntelliJ Idea: ** Choose **Import**. Navigate to the `pom.xml` file in the root of the downloaded package.

   For more information, see the related IDE documentation.

3. From your Java IDE, open `src/test/java/com.amazonaws.kinesisvideo.parser/examples/KinesisVideoRendererExampleTest`.

4. Remove the `@Ignore` directive from the file.

5. Update the `.stream` parameter with the name of your Kinesis video stream.

6. Run the `KinesisVideoRendererExample` test.

How It Works

Topics

- Sending MKV data
- Parsing MKV Fragments into Frames
- Decoding and Displaying the Frame

Sending MKV data

The example sends sample MKV data from the `rendering_example_video.mkv` file, using `PutMedia` to send video data to a stream named **render-example-stream**.

The application creates a `PutMediaWorker`:

```
1 PutMediaWorker putMediaWorker = PutMediaWorker.create(getRegion(),
2     getCredentialsProvider(),
3     getStreamName(),
4     inputStream,
5     streamOps.amazonKinesisVideo);
6 executorService.submit(putMediaWorker);
```

For information about the `PutMediaWorker` class, see Call PutMedia in the Stream Parser Library documentation.

Parsing MKV Fragments into Frames

The example then retrieves and parses the MKV fragments from the stream using a `GetMediaWorker`:

```
1 GetMediaWorker getMediaWorker = GetMediaWorker.create(getRegion(),
2     getCredentialsProvider(),
3     getStreamName(),
4     new StartSelector().withStartSelectorType(StartSelectorType.EARLIEST),
5     streamOps.amazonKinesisVideo,
6     getMediaProcessingArgumentsLocal.getFrameVisitor());
7 executorService.submit(getMediaWorker);
```

For more information about the `GetMediaWorker` class, see Call GetMedia in the Stream Parser Library documentation.

Decoding and Displaying the Frame

The example then decodes and displays the frame using JFrame.

The following code example is from the `KinesisVideoFrameViewer` class, which extends `JFrame`:

```
1  public void setImage(BufferedImage bufferedImage) {
2      image = bufferedImage;
3      repaint();
4  }
```

The image is displayed as an instance of java.awt.image.BufferedImage. For examples that show how to work with `BufferedImage`, see Reading/Loading an Image.

Monitoring Kinesis Video Streams

Monitoring is an important part of maintaining the reliability, availability, and performance of Kinesis Video Streams and your AWS solutions. You should collect monitoring data from all of the parts of your AWS solution so that you can more easily debug a multi-point failure if one occurs. Before you start monitoring Kinesis Video Streams, however, you should create a monitoring plan that includes answers to the following questions:

- What are your monitoring goals?
- What resources will you monitor?
- How often will you monitor these resources?
- What monitoring tools will you use?
- Who will perform the monitoring tasks?
- Who should be notified when something goes wrong?

After you have defined your monitoring goals and have created your monitoring plan, the next step is to establish a baseline for normal Kinesis Video Streams performance in your environment. You should measure Kinesis Video Streams performance at various times and under different load conditions. As you monitor Kinesis Video Streams, you should store a history of monitoring data that you've collected. You can compare current Kinesis Video Streams performance to this historical data to help you to identify normal performance patterns and performance anomalies, and devise methods to address issues that may arise.

Topics

- Monitoring Kinesis Video Streams Metrics with CloudWatch
- Logging Kinesis Video Streams API Calls with AWS CloudTrail

Monitoring Kinesis Video Streams Metrics with CloudWatch

You can monitor a Kinesis video stream using Amazon CloudWatch, which collects and processes raw data from Kinesis Video Streams into readable, near real-time metrics. These statistics are recorded for a period of 15 months, so that you can access historical information and gain a better perspective on how your web application or service is performing.

To access the CloudWatch dashboard for a Kinesis video stream, choose **View stream metrics in CloudWatch** in the **Stream info** section of the console page for the stream.

For a list of available metrics that Kinesis Video Streams supports, see Kinesis Video Streams Metrics and Dimensions.

CloudWatch Metrics Guidance

CloudWatch metrics can be useful for finding answers to the following questions:

Topics

- Is data reaching the Kinesis Video Streams service?
- Why is data not being successfully ingested by the Kinesis Video Streams service?
- Why can't the data be read from the Kinesis Video Streams service at the same rate as it's being sent from the producer?
- Why is there no video in the console, or why is the video being played with a delay?
- What is the delay in reading real-time data, and why is the client lagging behind the head of the stream?
- Is the client reading data out of the Kinesis video stream, and at what rate?
- Why can't the client read data out of the Kinesis video stream?

Is data reaching the Kinesis Video Streams service?

Relevant metrics:

- PutMedia.IncomingBytes
- PutMedia.IncomingFragments
- PutMedia.IncomingFrames

Action items:

- If there is a drop in these metrics, check if your application is still sending data to the service.
- Check the network bandwidth. If your network bandwidth is insufficient, it could be slowing down the rate the service is receiving the data.

Why is data not being successfully ingested by the Kinesis Video Streams service?

Relevant metrics:

- PutMedia.Requests
- PutMedia.ConnectionErrors
- PutMedia.Success
- PutMedia.ErrorAckCount

Action items:

- If there is an increase in PutMedia.ConnectionErrors, look at the HTTP response/error codes received by the producer client to see what errors are occurring while establishing the connection.

- If there is a drop in `PutMedia.Success` or increase in `PutMedia.ErrorAckCount`, look at the ack error code in the ack responses sent by the service to see why ingestion of data is failing. For more information, see AckErrorCode.Values.

Why can't the data be read from the Kinesis Video Streams service at the same rate as it's being sent from the producer?

Relevant metrics:

- `PutMedia.FragmentIngestionLatency`
- `PutMedia.IncomingBytes`

Action items:

- If there is a drop in these metrics, check the network bandwidth of your connections. Low-bandwidth connections could cause the data to reach the service at a lower rate.

Why is there no video in the console, or why is the video being played with a delay?

Relevant metrics:

- `PutMedia.FragmentIngestionLatency`
- `PutMedia.FragmentPersistLatency`
- `PutMedia.Success`
- `ListFragments.Latency`
- `PutMedia.IncomingFragments`

Action items:

- If there is an increase in `PutMedia.FragmentIngestionLatency` or a drop in `PutMedia.IncomingFragments`, check the network bandwidth and whether the data is still being sent.
- If there is a drop in `PutMedia.Success`, check the ack error codes. For more information, see AckError-Code.Values.
- If there is an increase in `PutMedia.FragmentPersistLatency` or `ListFragments.Latency`, you are most likely experiencing a service issue. If the condition persists for an extended period of time, check with your customer service contact to see if there is an issue with your service.

What is the delay in reading real-time data, and why is the client lagging behind the head of the stream?

Relevant metrics:

- `GetMedia.MillisBehindNow`
- `GetMedia.ConnectionErrors`
- `GetMedia.Success`

Action items:

- If there is an increase in `GetMedia.ConnectionErrors`, then the consumer might be falling behind in reading the stream, due to frequent attempts to re-connect to the stream. Look at the HTTP response/error codes returned for the `GetMedia` request.
- If there is a drop in `GetMedia.Success`, then it's likely due to the service being unable to send the data to the consumer, which would result in dropped connection, and reconnects from consumers, which would result in the consumer lagging behind the head of the stream.
- If there is an increase in `GetMedia.MillisBehindNow`, look at your bandwidth limits to see if you are receiving the data at a slower rate because of lower bandwidth.

Is the client reading data out of the Kinesis video stream, and at what rate?

Relevant metrics:

- GetMedia.OutgoingBytes
- GetMedia.OutgoingFragments
- GetMedia.OutgoingFrames
- GetMediaForFragmentList.OutgoingBytes
- GetMediaForFragmentList.OutgoingFragments
- GetMediaForFragmentList.OutgoingFrames

Action items:

- These metrics indicate what rate real-time and archived data is being read.

Why can't the client read data out of the Kinesis video stream?

Relevant metrics:

- GetMedia.ConnectionErrors
- GetMedia.Success
- GetMediaForFragmentList.Success
- PutMedia.IncomingBytes

Action items:

- If there is an increase in GetMedia.ConnectionErrors, look at the HTTP response/error codes returned by the GetMedia request. For more information, see AckErrorCode.Values.
- If you are trying to read the latest/live data, check PutMedia.IncomingBytes to see if there is data coming into the stream for the service to send to the consumers.
- If there is a drop in GetMedia.Success or GetMediaForFragmentList.Success, it's likely due to the service being unable to send the data to the consumer. If the condition persists for an extended period of time, check with your customer service contact to see if there is an issue with your service.

Logging Kinesis Video Streams API Calls with AWS CloudTrail

Amazon Kinesis Video Streams is integrated with AWS CloudTrail, which captures API calls made by or on behalf of Kinesis Video Streams. CloudTrail then delivers the log files to the Amazon Simple Storage Service (Amazon S3) bucket that you specify. You can make the API calls indirectly through the Kinesis Video Streams console, or directly by using the Kinesis Video Streams API. You can use the information collected by CloudTrail to determine what request was made to Kinesis Video Streams, the source IP address from which the request was made, who made the request, when it was made, and so on. To learn more about CloudTrail, including how to configure and enable it, see the *AWS CloudTrail User Guide*.

Kinesis Video Streams and CloudTrail

CloudTrail logging is enabled by default. Calls made to Kinesis Video Streams actions are tracked in log files. Records for Kinesis Video Streams are written in a log file, together with records from any other AWS service that is enabled for CloudTrail logging. CloudTrail determines when to create and write to a new file based on the specified time period and file size.

The following actions are supported:

- CreateStream
- DeleteStream
- DescribeStream
- GetDataEndpoint
- ListStreams
- ListTagsForStream
- TagStream
- UntagStream
- UpdateDataRetention
- UpdateStream

Each log entry contains information about who generated the request. For example, if a request is made to create a stream (CreateStream), the user identity of the person or service that made the request is logged. The user identity information helps you determine whether the request was made with root or IAM user credentials, with temporary security credentials for a role or federated user, or by another AWS service. For more information, see the userIdentity element in the *AWS CloudTrail User Guide*.

You can store your log files in your bucket for as long as you need to, but you can also define Amazon S3 lifecycle rules to archive or delete log files automatically. By default, your log files are encrypted with Amazon S3 server-side encryption (SSE).

You can also aggregate Kinesis Video Streams log files from multiple AWS Regions and multiple AWS accounts into a single Amazon S3 bucket. For more information, see Aggregating CloudTrail Log Files to a Single Amazon S3 Bucket in the *AWS CloudTrail User Guide*.

You can have CloudTrail publish Amazon Simple Notification Service (Amazon SNS) notifications when new log files are delivered if you want to take quick action upon log file delivery. For more information, see Configuring Amazon SNS Notifications in the *AWS CloudTrail User Guide*.

Log File Entries for Kinesis Video Streams

CloudTrail log files can contain one or more log entries, where each entry is made up of multiple JSON-formatted events. A log entry represents a single request from any source and includes information about the requested action, any parameters, the date and time of the action, and so on. The log entries are not guaranteed to be in any particular order. That is, this is not an ordered stack trace of API calls.

The following is an example CloudTrail log entry.

```
 1  {
 2      "Records": [
 3          {
 4              "eventVersion": "1.05",
 5              "userIdentity": {
 6                  "type": "IAMUser",
 7                  "principalId": "EX_PRINCIPAL_ID",
 8                  "arn": "arn:aws:iam::123456789012:user/Alice",
 9                  "accountId": "123456789012",
10                  "accessKeyId": "EXAMPLE_KEY_ID",
11                  "userName": "Alice"
12              },
13              "eventTime": "2018-05-25T00:16:31Z",
14              "eventSource": " kinesisvideo.amazonaws.com",
15              "eventName": "CreateStream",
16              "awsRegion": "us-east-1",
17              "sourceIPAddress": "127.0.0.1",
18              "userAgent": "aws-sdk-java/unknown-version Linux/x.xx",
19              "requestParameters": {
20                  "streamName": "VideoStream",
21                  "dataRetentionInHours": 2,
22                  "mediaType": "mediaType",
23                  "kmsKeyId": "arn:aws:kms::us-east-1:123456789012:alias",
24      "deviceName": "my-device"
25              },
26              "responseElements": {
27      "streamARN":arn:aws:kinesisvideo:us-east-1:123456789012:stream/VideoStream"/12345
28              },
29              "requestID": "db6c59f8-c757-11e3-bc3b-57923b443c1c",
30              "eventID": "b7acfcd0-6ca9-4ee1-a3d7-c4e8d420d99b"
31          },
32          {
33              "eventVersion": "1.05",
34              "userIdentity": {
35                  "type": "IAMUser",
36                  "principalId": "EX_PRINCIPAL_ID",
37                  "arn": "arn:aws:iam::123456789012:user/Alice",
38                  "accountId": "123456789012",
39                  "accessKeyId": "EXAMPLE_KEY_ID",
40                  "userName": "Alice"
41              },
42              "eventTime": "2018-05-25:17:06Z",
43              "eventSource": " kinesisvideo.amazonaws."com,
44              "eventName": "DeleteStream",
45              "awsRegion": "us-east-1",
46              "sourceIPAddress": "127.0.0.1",
47              "userAgent": "aws-sdk-java/unknown-version Linux/x.xx",
48              "requestParameters": {
49                  "streamARN": "arn:aws:kinesisvideo:us-east-1:012345678910:stream/VideoStream
                        /12345",
50                  "currentVersion": "keqrjeqkj9"
51              },
52              "responseElements": null,
53              "requestID": "f0944d86-c757-11e3-b4ae-25654b1d3136",
```

```
54              "eventID": "0b2f1396-88af-4561-b16f-398f8eaea596"
55          },
56          {
57              "eventVersion": "1.05",
58              "userIdentity": {
59                  "type": "IAMUser",
60                  "principalId": "EX_PRINCIPAL_ID",
61                  "arn": "arn:aws:iam::123456789012:user/Alice",
62                  "accountId": "123456789012",
63                  "accessKeyId": "EXAMPLE_KEY_ID",
64                  "userName": "Alice"
65              },
66              "eventTime": "2014-04-19T00:15:02Z",
67              "eventSource": " kinesisvideo.amazonaws."com,
68              "eventName": "DescribeStream",
69              "awsRegion": "us-east-1",
70              "sourceIPAddress": "127.0.0.1",
71              "userAgent": "aws-sdk-java/unknown-version Linux/x.xx",
72              "requestParameters": {
73                  "streamName": "VideoStream"
74               },
75              "responseElements": null,
76              "requestID": "a68541ca-c757-11e3-901b-cbcfe5b3677a",
77              "eventID": "22a5fb8f-4e61-4bee-a8ad-3b72046b4c4d"
78          },
79          {
80              "eventVersion": "1.05",
81              "userIdentity": {
82                  "type": "IAMUser",
83                  "principalId": "EX_PRINCIPAL_ID",
84                  "arn": "arn:aws:iam::123456789012:user/Alice",
85                  "accountId": "123456789012",
86                  "accessKeyId": "EXAMPLE_KEY_ID",
87                  "userName": "Alice"
88              },
89              "eventTime": "2014-04-19T00:15:03Z",
90              "eventSource": "kinesisvideo.amazonaws.com",
91              "eventName": "GetDataEndpoint",
92              "awsRegion": "us-east-1",
93              "sourceIPAddress": "127.0.0.1",
94              "userAgent": "aws-sdk-java/unknown-version Linux/x.xx",
95              "requestParameters": {
96                  "streamName": "VideoStream",
97                  "aPIName": "LIST_FRAGMENTS"
98  "
99               },
100             "responseElements": null,
101             "requestID": "a6e6e9cd-c757-11e3-901b-cbcfe5b3677a",
102             "eventID": "dcd2126f-c8d2-4186-b32a-192dd48d7e33"
103         },
104         {
105             "eventVersion": "1.05",
106             "userIdentity": {
107                 "type": "IAMUser",
```

```
108              "principalId": "EX_PRINCIPAL_ID",
109              "arn": "arn:aws:iam::123456789012:user/Alice",
110              "accountId": "123456789012",
111              "accessKeyId": "EXAMPLE_KEY_ID",
112              "userName": "Alice"
113          },
114          "eventTime": "2018-05-25T00:16:56Z",
115          "eventSource": "kinesisvideo.amazonaws.com",
116          "eventName": "ListStreams",
117          "awsRegion": "us-east-1",
118          "sourceIPAddress": "127.0.0.1",
119          "userAgent": "aws-sdk-java/unknown-version Linux/x.xx",
120          "requestParameters": {
121              "maxResults": 100,
122              "streamNameCondition": {"comparisonValue":""MyVideoStream comparisonOperator":"
                    BEGINS_WITH"}}
123          },
124          "responseElements": null,
125          "requestID": "e9f9c8eb-c757-11e3-bf1d-6948db3cd570",
126          "eventID": "77cf0d06-ce90-42da-9576-71986fec411f"
127      }
128   ]
129 }
```

135

Kinesis Video Streams Limits

Kinesis Video Streams has the following limits:

The limits below are either soft [s], which can be upgraded by submitting a support ticket, or hard [h], which cannot be increased.

Control Plane API limits

The following section describes limits for Control Plane APIs.

When an account-level Request limit is reached, a `ClientLimitExceededException` is thrown.

When an account-level Streams limit is reached, or a stream-level limit is reached, a `StreamLimitExceededException` is thrown.

Control Plane API limits

API	Account Limit: Request	Account Limit: Streams	Stream-level limit	Relevant Exceptions and Notes
CreateStream	50 TPS [s]	100 streams per account [s]	5 TPS [h]	Devices, CLIs, SDK-driven access and the console can all invoke this API. Only one API call succeeds if the stream doesn't already exist.
DescribeStream	300 TPS [h]	N/A	5 TPS [h]	
UpdateStream	50 TPS [h]	N/A	5 TPS [h]	
ListStreams	300 TPS [h]	N/A	5 TPS [h]	
DeleteStream	50 TPS [h]	N/A	5 TPS [h]	
GetDataEndpoint	300 TPS [h]	N/A	5 TPS [h]	When combined with account limit, this implies a maximum of 60 streams can be Put to and Read from (with 4 consumers).

Media and Archived Media API limits

The following section describes limits for Media and Archived Media APIs.

When a stream-level limit is exceeded, a `StreamLimitExceededException` is thrown.

When a connection-level limit is reached, a `ConnectionLimitExceededException` is thrown.

The following errors or acks are thrown when a fragment-level limit is reached:

- A `MIN_FRAGMENT_DURATION_REACHED` ack is returned for a fragment below the minumum duration.
- A `MAX_FRAGMENT_DURATION_REACHED` ack is returned for a fragment above the maximum duration.
- A `MAX_FRAGMENT_SIZE` ack is returned for a fragment above the maximum data size.

- A `FragmentLimitExceeded` exception is thrown if a fragment limit is reached in a `GetMediaForFragmentList` operation.

Data Plane API limits

API	Stream-level limit	Connection-level limit	Bandwidth limit	Fragment-level limit	Relevant Exceptions and Notes
PutMedia	5 TPS [h]	1 [s]	12.5 MB/second, or 100 Mbps [s]	[See the AWS documentation website for more details]	A typical PutMedia request will contain data for several seconds, resulting in a lower TPS per stream. In the case of multiple concurrent connections that exceed limits, the last connection is accepted.

API	Stream-level limit	Connection-level limit	Bandwidth limit	Fragment-level limit	Relevant Exceptions and Notes
GetMedia	5 TPS [h]	3 [s]	25 MB/s or 200 Mbps [s]	N/A	Only three clients can concurrently receive content from the media stream at any moment of time. Further client connections are rejected. A unique consuming client shouldn't need more than 2 or 3 TPS, since once the connection is established, we anticipate that the application will read continuously. If a typical fragment is approximately 5 MB, this limit will mean ~75 MB/ sec per Kinesis video stream. Such a stream would have an outgoing bit rate of 2x the streams' maximum incoming bit rate.
ListFragments	5 TPS [h]	5 [s]	N/A	N/A	Five fragment-based consuming applications can concurrently list fragments based on processing requirements.

API	Stream-level limit	Connection-level limit	Bandwidth limit	Fragment-level limit	Relevant Exceptions and Notes
GetMediaFor-FragmentList	5 TPS [h]	5 [s]	25 MB/s or 200 MbpsA [s]	Maximum number of fragments: 1000 [h]	Five fragment-based consuming applications can concurrently get media. Further connections are rejected.

Troubleshooting Kinesis Video Streams

Use the following information to troubleshoot common issues encountered with Amazon Kinesis Video Streams.

Topics

- Troubleshooting General Issues
- Troubleshooting API Issues
- Troubleshooting Java Issues
- Troubleshooting Producer Library Issues
- Troubleshooting Stream Parser Library Issues

Troubleshooting General Issues

This section describes general issues that you might encounter when working with Kinesis Video Streams.

Topics

- Latency too high

Latency too high

Latency might be caused by the duration of fragments that are sent to the Kinesis Video Streams service. One way to reduce the latency between the producer and the service is to configure the media pipeline to produce shorter fragment durations.

To reduce the number of frames sent in each fragment, and thus reduce the amount of time for each fragment, reduce the following value in **kinesis_video_gstreamer_sample_app.cpp**:

```
1 g_object_set(G_OBJECT (data.encoder), "bframes", 0, "key-int-max", 45, "bitrate", 512, NULL);
```

Troubleshooting API Issues

This section describes API issues that you might encounter when working with Kinesis Video Streams.

Topics

- Error: "Unable to determine service/operation name to be authorized"
- Error: "Failed to put a frame in the stream"
- Error: "Service closed connection before final AckEvent was received"
- Error: "STATUS_STORE_OUT_OF_MEMORY"

Error: "Unable to determine service/operation name to be authorized"

GetMedia can fail with the following error:

```
1 Unable to determine service/operation name to be authorized
```

This error might occur if the endpoint is not properly specified. When you are getting the endpoint, be sure to include the following parameter in the **GetDataEndpoint** call, depending on the API to be called:

```
1 --api-name GET_MEDIA
2 --api-name PUT_MEDIA
3 --api-name GET_MEDIA_FOR_FRAGMENT_LIST
4 --api-name LIST_FRAGMENTS
```

Error: "Failed to put a frame in the stream"

`PutMedia` can fail with the following error:

```
1 Failed to put a frame in the stream
```

This error might occur if connectivity or permissions are not available to the service. Run the following in the AWS CLI, and verify that the stream information can be retrieved:

```
1 aws kinesisvideo describe-stream --stream-name StreamName --endpoint https://ServiceEndpoint.
    kinesisvideo.region.amazonaws.com
```

If the call fails, see Troubleshooting AWS CLI Errors for more information.

Error: "Service closed connection before final AckEvent was received"

`PutMedia` can fail with the following error:

```
1 com.amazonaws.SdkClientException: Service closed connection before final AckEvent was received
```

This error might occur if `PushbackInputStream` is improperly implemented. Ensure that the `unread()` methods are correctly implemented.

Error: "STATUS_STORE_OUT_OF_MEMORY"

`PutMedia` can fail with the following error:

```
1 The content store is out of memory.
```

This error occurs when the content store is not allocated with sufficient size. To increase the size of the content store, increase the value of `StorageInfo.storageSize`. For more information, see StorageInfo.

Troubleshooting Java Issues

This section describes how to troubleshoot common Java issues encountered when working with Kinesis Video Streams.

Topics

- Enabling Java logs

Enabling Java logs

To troubleshoot issues with Java samples and libraries, it is helpful to enable and examine the debug logs. To enable debug logs, do the following:

1. Add `log4j` to the `pom.xml``` file, in the`dependencies' node:

```
1 <dependency>
2     <groupId>log4j</groupId>
3     <artifactId>log4j</artifactId>
4     <version>1.2.17</version>
5 </dependency>
```

2. In the `target/classes` directory, create a file named `log4j.properties` with the following contents:

```
1 # Root logger option
2 log4j.rootLogger=DEBUG, stdout
3
4 # Redirect log messages to console
5 log4j.appender.stdout=org.apache.log4j.ConsoleAppender
6 log4j.appender.stdout.Target=System.out
7 log4j.appender.stdout.layout=org.apache.log4j.PatternLayout
8 log4j.appender.stdout.layout.ConversionPattern=%d{yyyy-MM-dd HH:mm:ss} %-5p %c{1}:%L - %m%n
9
10 log4j.logger.org.apache.http.wire=DEBUG
```

The debug logs then print to the IDE console.

Troubleshooting Producer Library Issues

This section describes issues that you might encounter when using the Producer Libraries.

Topics

- Cannot compile the Producer SDK
- Video stream does not appear in the console
- Error: "Security token included in the request is invalid" when streaming data using the GStreamer demo application
- Error: "Failed to submit frame to Kinesis Video client"
- GStreamer application stops with "streaming stopped, reason not-negotiated" message on OS X
- Error: "Failed to allocate heap" when creating Kinesis Video Client in GStreamer demo on Raspberry Pi
- Error: "Illegal Instruction" when running GStreamer demo on Raspberry Pi
- Camera fails to load on Raspberry Pi
- Camera can't be found on macOS High Sierra
- jni.h file not found when compiling on macOS High Sierra
- Curl errors when running the GStreamer demo app
- Time stamp/range assertion at run time on Raspberry Pi
- Assertion on gst_value_set_fraction_range_full on Raspberry Pi

Cannot compile the Producer SDK

Verify that the required libraries are in your path. To verify this, use the following command:

```
1 $ env | grep LD_LIBRARY_PATH
2 LD_LIBRARY_PATH=/home/local/awslabs/amazon-kinesis-video-streams-producer-sdk-cpp/kinesis-video-
      native-build/downloads/local/lib
```

Video stream does not appear in the console

To display your video stream in the console, it must be encoded using H.264 in AvCC format. If your stream is not displayed, verify the following:

- Your NAL Adaptation Flags are set to NAL_ADAPTATION_ANNEXB_NALS | NAL_ADAPTATION_ANNEXB_CPD_NALS if the original stream is in Annex-B format. This is the default value in the StreamDefinition constructor.

- You are providing the codec private data correctly. For H.264, this is the sequence parameter set (SPS) and picture parameter set (PPS). Depending on your media source, this data may be retrieved from the media source separately or encoded into the frame.

Many elementary streams are in the following format, where `Ab` is the Annex-B start code (001 or 0001):

```
1 Ab(Sps)Ab(Pps)Ab(I-frame)Ab(P/B-frame) Ab(P/B-frame)…. Ab(Sps)Ab(Pps)Ab(I-frame)Ab(P/B-
    frame) Ab(P/B-frame)
```

The CPD (Codec Private Data) which in the case of H.264 is in the stream as SPS and PPS, can be adapted to the AvCC format. Unless the media pipeline gives the CPD separately, the application can extract the CPD from the frame by looking for the first Idr frame (which should contain the SPS/PPS), extract the two NALUs [which will be Ab(Sps)Ab(Pps)] and set it in the CPD in `StreamDefinition`.

Error: "Security token included in the request is invalid" when streaming data using the GStreamer demo application

If this error occurs, there is an issue with your credentials. Verify the following:

- If you are using temporary credentials, you must specify the session token.
- Verify that your temporary credentials are not expired.
- Verify that you have the proper rights set up.
- On macOS, verify that you do not have credentials cached in Keychain.

Error: "Failed to submit frame to Kinesis Video client"

If this error occurs, the time stamps are not properly set in the source stream. Try the following:

- Use the latest SDK sample, which might have an update that fixes your issue.
- Set the high-quality stream to a higher bit rate, and fix any jitter in the source stream if the camera supports doing so.

GStreamer application stops with "streaming stopped, reason not-negotiated" message on OS X

Streaming may stop on OS X with the following message:

```
1 Debugging information: gstbasesrc.c(2939): void gst_base_src_loop(GstPad *) (): /GstPipeline:
    test-pipeline/GstAutoVideoSrc:source/GstAVFVideoSrc:source-actual-src-avfvide:
2 streaming stopped, reason not-negotiated (-4)
```

A possible workaround for this is to remove the framerate parameters from the `gst_caps_new_simple` call in `kinesis_video_gstreamer_sample_app.cpp`:

```
1 GstCaps *h264_caps = gst_caps_new_simple("video/x-h264",
2                                          "profile", G_TYPE_STRING, "baseline",
3                                          "stream-format", G_TYPE_STRING, "avc",
4                                          "alignment", G_TYPE_STRING, "au",
5                                          "width", GST_TYPE_INT_RANGE, 320, 1920,
6                                          "height", GST_TYPE_INT_RANGE, 240, 1080,
7                                          "framerate", GST_TYPE_FRACTION_RANGE, 0, 1, 30, 1,
8                                          NULL);
```

Error: "Failed to allocate heap" when creating Kinesis Video Client in GStreamer demo on Raspberry Pi

The GStreamer sample application tries to allocate 512 MB of RAM, which might not be available on your system. You can reduce this allocation by reducing the following value in `KinesisVideoProducer.cpp`:

```
1 device_info.storageInfo.storageSize = 512 * 1024 * 1024;
```

Error: "Illegal Instruction" when running GStreamer demo on Raspberry Pi

If you encounter the following error when executing the GStreamer demo, ensure that you have compiled the application for the correct version of your device. (For example, ensure that you are not compiling for Raspberry Pi 3 when you are running on Raspberry Pi 2.)

```
1 INFO - Initializing curl.
2 Illegal instruction
```

Camera fails to load on Raspberry Pi

To check whether the camera is loaded, run the following:

```
1 $ ls /dev/video*
```

If nothing is found, run the following:

```
1 $ vcgencmd get_camera
```

The output should look similar to the following:

```
1 supported=1 detected=1
```

If the driver does not detect the camera, do the following:

1. Check the physical camera setup and verify that it's connected properly.
2. Run the following to upgrade the firmware:

   ```
   1 $ sudo rpi-update
   ```

3. Restart the device.
4. Run the following to load the driver:

   ```
   1 $ sudo modprobe bcm2835-v4l2
   ```

5. Verify that the camera was detected:

   ```
   1 $ ls /dev/video*
   ```

Camera can't be found on macOS High Sierra

On macOS High Sierra, the demo application can't find the camera if more than one camera is available.

jni.h file not found when compiling on macOS High Sierra

To resolve this error, update your installation of Xcode to the latest version.

Curl errors when running the GStreamer demo app

To resolve curl errors when you run the GStreamer demo application, copy this certificate file to `/etc/ssl/cert.pem`.

Time stamp/range assertion at run time on Raspberry Pi

If a time stamp range assertion occurs at run time, update the firmware and restart the device:

```
1 $ sudo rpi-update
2 $ sudo reboot
```

Assertion on gst_value_set_fraction_range_full on Raspberry Pi

The following assertion appears if the uv4l service is running:

```
1 gst_util_fraction_compare (numerator_start, denominator_start, numerator_end, denominator_end) <
      0' failed
```

If this occurs, stop the uv4l service and restart the application.

Troubleshooting Stream Parser Library Issues

This section describes issues that you might encounter when using the Stream Parser Library.

Topics

- Cannot access a single frame from the stream
- Fragment decoding error

Cannot access a single frame from the stream

To access a single frame from a streaming source in your consumer application, ensure that your stream contains the correct codec private data. For information about the format of the data in a stream, see Data Model.

To learn how to use codec private data to access a frame, see the following test file on the GitHub website: KinesisVideoRendererExampleTest.java

Fragment decoding error

If your fragments are not properly encoded in an H.264 format and level that the browser supports, you might see the following error when playing your stream in the console:

```
1 Fragment Decoding Error
2 There was an error decoding the video data. Verify that the stream contains valid H.264 content
```

If this occurs, verify the following:

- The resolution of the frames matches the resolution specified in the Codec Private Data.
- The H.264 profile and level of the encoded frames matches the profile and level specified in the Codec Private Data.
- The browser supports the profile/level combination. Most current browsers support all profile and level combinations.
- The time stamps are accurate and in the correct order, and no duplicate time stamps are being created.
- Your application is encoding the frame data using the H.264 format.

145

Document History for Amazon Kinesis Video Streams

The following table describes the important changes to the documentation since the last release of Amazon Kinesis Video Streams.

- **Latest API version:** 2017-11-29
- **Latest documentation update:** June 20, 2018

Change	Description	Date
Streaming from an RTSP Source	Sample application for Kinesis Video Streams that runs in a Docker container and streams video from an RTSP source. For more information, see RTSP and Docker.	June 20, 2018
C++ Producer SDK GStreamer Plugin	Shows how to build the C++ Producer Library to use as a GStreamer destination. For more information, see GStreamer Plugin.	June 15, 2018
Producer SDK callbacks reference documentation	Reference documentation for the callbacks used by the Kinesis Video Streams Producer Libraries. For more information, see Producer SDK Callbacks.	June 12, 2018
System requirements	Documentation for memory and storage requirements for producer devices and SDK. For more information, see Kinesis Video Streams System Requirements.	May 30, 2018
CloudTrail support	Documentation for using CloudTrail to monitor API usage. For more information, see Logging Kinesis Video Streams API Calls with AWS CloudTrail.	May 24, 2018
Producer SDK structures reference documentation	Reference documentation for the structures used by the Kinesis Video Streams Producer Libraries. For more information, see Producer SDK Structures and Kinesis Video Stream Structures.	May 7, 2018
Renderer example documentation	Documentation for the Renderer example application, which shows how to decode and display frames from a Kinesis video stream. For more information, see Example: Parsing and Rendering Kinesis Video Streams Fragments.	Mar 15, 2018

Change	Description	Date
Producer SDK Limits reference documentation	Information about limits for operations in the C++ Producer Library. For more information, see Producer SDK Limits.	Mar 13, 2018
C++ Producer SDK for Raspberry Pi	Procedure for setting up and running the C++ Producer Library on a Raspberry Pi device. For more information, see Using the C++ Producer SDK on Raspberry Pi.	Mar 13, 2018
Monitoring	Information about monitoring Kinesis Video Streams metrics and API calls using Amazon CloudWatch and AWS CloudTrail. For more information, see Monitoring Kinesis Video Streams.	February 5, 2018
Network Abstraction Layer (NAL) adaptation flag reference	Information about setting NAL adaptation flags when consuming streaming video. For more information, see NAL Adaptation Flags.	January 15, 2018
Android support for streaming video	Kinesis Video Streams now supports streaming video from Android devices. For more information, see Android Producer Library.	January 12, 2018
Kinesis Video example documentation	Documentation for the Kinesis Video example application, which shows how to use the Kinesis Video Stream Parser Library in an application. For more information, see KinesisVideoExample.	January 9, 2018
GStreamer example documentation	Documentation for the GStreamer example application that is included in the C++ Producer SDK. For more information, see Example: Using GStreamer with Kinesis Video Streams.	January 5, 2018
Kinesis Video Streams documentation released	This is the initial release of the Amazon Kinesis Video Streams Developer Guide.	November 29, 2017

API Reference

This section contains the API Reference documentation.

Actions

The following actions are supported by Amazon Kinesis Video Streams:

- CreateStream
- DeleteStream
- DescribeStream
- GetDataEndpoint
- ListStreams
- ListTagsForStream
- TagStream
- UntagStream
- UpdateDataRetention
- UpdateStream

The following actions are supported by Amazon Kinesis Video Streams Media:

- GetMedia
- PutMedia

The following actions are supported by Amazon Kinesis Video Streams Archived Media:

- GetHLSStreamingSessionURL
- GetMediaForFragmentList
- ListFragments

Amazon Kinesis Video Streams

The following data types are supported by Amazon Kinesis Video Streams:

- StreamInfo
- StreamNameCondition

CreateStream

Creates a new Kinesis video stream.

When you create a new stream, Kinesis Video Streams assigns it a version number. When you change the stream's metadata, Kinesis Video Streams updates the version.

`CreateStream` is an asynchronous operation.

For information about how the service works, see How it Works.

You must have permissions for the `KinesisVideo:CreateStream` action.

Request Syntax

```
1  POST /createStream HTTP/1.1
2  Content-type: application/json
3
4  {
5     "[DataRetentionInHours](#KinesisVideo-CreateStream-request-DataRetentionInHours)": number,
6     "[DeviceName](#KinesisVideo-CreateStream-request-DeviceName)": "string",
7     "[KmsKeyId](#KinesisVideo-CreateStream-request-KmsKeyId)": "string",
8     "[MediaType](#KinesisVideo-CreateStream-request-MediaType)": "string",
9     "[StreamName](#KinesisVideo-CreateStream-request-StreamName)": "string"
10 }
```

URI Request Parameters

The request does not use any URI parameters.

Request Body

The request accepts the following data in JSON format.

** DataRetentionInHours ** The number of hours that you want to retain the data in the stream. Kinesis Video Streams retains the data in a data store that is associated with the stream.
The default value is 0, indicating that the stream does not persist data.
When the `DataRetentionInHours` value is 0, consumers can still consume the fragments that remain in the service host buffer, which has a retention time limit of 5 minutes and a retention memory limit of 200 MB. Fragments are removed from the buffer when either limit is reached.
Type: Integer
Valid Range: Minimum value of 0.
Required: No

** DeviceName ** The name of the device that is writing to the stream.
In the current implementation, Kinesis Video Streams does not use this name. Type: String
Length Constraints: Minimum length of 1. Maximum length of 128.
Pattern: `[a-zA-Z0-9_.-]+`
Required: No

** KmsKeyId ** The ID of the AWS Key Management Service (AWS KMS) key that you want Kinesis Video Streams to use to encrypt stream data.
If no key ID is specified, the default, Kinesis Video-managed key (`aws/kinesisvideo`) is used.
For more information, see DescribeKey.
Type: String

Length Constraints: Minimum length of 1. Maximum length of 2048.
Required: No

** MediaType ** The media type of the stream. Consumers of the stream can use this information when processing the stream. For more information about media types, see Media Types. If you choose to specify the MediaType, see Naming Requirements for guidelines.
To play video on the console, the media must be H.264 encoded, and you need to specify this video type in this parameter as video/h264.
This parameter is optional; the default value is null (or empty in JSON).
Type: String
Length Constraints: Minimum length of 1. Maximum length of 128.
Pattern: [\w\-\.\+]+/[\w\-\.\+]+
Required: No

** StreamName ** A name for the stream that you are creating.
The stream name is an identifier for the stream, and must be unique for each account and region.
Type: String
Length Constraints: Minimum length of 1. Maximum length of 256.
Pattern: [a-zA-Z0-9_.-]+
Required: Yes

Response Syntax

```
1 HTTP/1.1 200
2 Content-type: application/json
3
4 {
5    "[StreamARN](#KinesisVideo-CreateStream-response-StreamARN)": "string"
6 }
```

Response Elements

If the action is successful, the service sends back an HTTP 200 response.

The following data is returned in JSON format by the service.

** StreamARN ** The Amazon Resource Name (ARN) of the stream.
Type: String
Length Constraints: Minimum length of 1. Maximum length of 1024.
Pattern: arn:aws:kinesisvideo:[a-z0-9-]+:[0-9]+:[a-z]+/[a-zA-Z0-9_.-]+/[0-9]+

Errors

For information about the errors that are common to all actions, see Common Errors.

AccountStreamLimitExceededException
The number of streams created for the account is too high.
HTTP Status Code: 400

ClientLimitExceededException
Kinesis Video Streams has throttled the request because you have exceeded the limit of allowed client calls. Try making the call later.
HTTP Status Code: 400

DeviceStreamLimitExceededException
Not implemented.
HTTP Status Code: 400

InvalidArgumentException
The value for this input parameter is invalid.
HTTP Status Code: 400

InvalidDeviceException
Not implemented.
HTTP Status Code: 400

ResourceInUseException
The stream is currently not available for this operation.
HTTP Status Code: 400

See Also

For more information about using this API in one of the language-specific AWS SDKs, see the following:

- AWS Command Line Interface
- AWS SDK for .NET
- AWS SDK for C++
- AWS SDK for Go
- AWS SDK for Java
- AWS SDK for JavaScript
- AWS SDK for PHP V3
- AWS SDK for Python
- AWS SDK for Ruby V2

DeleteStream

Deletes a Kinesis video stream and the data contained in the stream.

This method marks the stream for deletion, and makes the data in the stream inaccessible immediately.

To ensure that you have the latest version of the stream before deleting it, you can specify the stream version. Kinesis Video Streams assigns a version to each stream. When you update a stream, Kinesis Video Streams assigns a new version number. To get the latest stream version, use the `DescribeStream` API.

This operation requires permission for the `KinesisVideo:DeleteStream` action.

Request Syntax

```
1 POST /deleteStream HTTP/1.1
2 Content-type: application/json
3
4 {
5    "[CurrentVersion](#KinesisVideo-DeleteStream-request-CurrentVersion)": "string",
6    "[StreamARN](#KinesisVideo-DeleteStream-request-StreamARN)": "string"
7 }
```

URI Request Parameters

The request does not use any URI parameters.

Request Body

The request accepts the following data in JSON format.

** CurrentVersion ** Optional: The version of the stream that you want to delete.
Specify the version as a safeguard to ensure that your are deleting the correct stream. To get the stream version, use the `DescribeStream` API.
If not specified, only the `CreationTime` is checked before deleting the stream.
Type: String
Length Constraints: Minimum length of 1. Maximum length of 64.
Pattern: `[a-zA-Z0-9]+`
Required: No

** StreamARN ** The Amazon Resource Name (ARN) of the stream that you want to delete.
Type: String
Length Constraints: Minimum length of 1. Maximum length of 1024.
Pattern: `arn:aws:kinesisvideo:[a-z0-9-]+:[0-9]+:[a-z]+/[a-zA-Z0-9_.-]+/[0-9]+`
Required: Yes

Response Syntax

```
1 HTTP/1.1 200
```

Response Elements

If the action is successful, the service sends back an HTTP 200 response with an empty HTTP body.

Errors

For information about the errors that are common to all actions, see Common Errors.

ClientLimitExceededException
Kinesis Video Streams has throttled the request because you have exceeded the limit of allowed client calls. Try making the call later.
HTTP Status Code: 400

InvalidArgumentException
The value for this input parameter is invalid.
HTTP Status Code: 400

NotAuthorizedException
The caller is not authorized to perform this operation.
HTTP Status Code: 401

ResourceNotFoundException
Amazon Kinesis Video Streams can't find the stream that you specified.
HTTP Status Code: 404

See Also

For more information about using this API in one of the language-specific AWS SDKs, see the following:

- AWS Command Line Interface
- AWS SDK for .NET
- AWS SDK for C++
- AWS SDK for Go
- AWS SDK for Java
- AWS SDK for JavaScript
- AWS SDK for PHP V3
- AWS SDK for Python
- AWS SDK for Ruby V2

DescribeStream

Returns the most current information about the specified stream. You must specify either the `StreamName` or the `StreamARN`.

Request Syntax

```
1  POST /describeStream HTTP/1.1
2  Content-type: application/json
3
4  {
5     "[StreamARN](#KinesisVideo-DescribeStream-request-StreamARN)": "string",
6     "[StreamName](#KinesisVideo-DescribeStream-request-StreamName)": "string"
7  }
```

URI Request Parameters

The request does not use any URI parameters.

Request Body

The request accepts the following data in JSON format.

** StreamARN ** The Amazon Resource Name (ARN) of the stream.
Type: String
Length Constraints: Minimum length of 1. Maximum length of 1024.
Pattern: `arn:aws:kinesisvideo:[a-z0-9-]+:[0-9]+:[a-z]+/[a-zA-Z0-9_.-]+/[0-9]+`
Required: No

** StreamName ** The name of the stream.
Type: String
Length Constraints: Minimum length of 1. Maximum length of 256.
Pattern: `[a-zA-Z0-9_.-]+`
Required: No

Response Syntax

```
1  HTTP/1.1 200
2  Content-type: application/json
3
4  {
5     "[StreamInfo](#KinesisVideo-DescribeStream-response-StreamInfo)": {
6        "[CreationTime](API_StreamInfo.md#KinesisVideo-Type-StreamInfo-CreationTime)": number,
7        "[DataRetentionInHours](API_StreamInfo.md#KinesisVideo-Type-StreamInfo-
              DataRetentionInHours)": number,
8        "[DeviceName](API_StreamInfo.md#KinesisVideo-Type-StreamInfo-DeviceName)": "string",
9        "[KmsKeyId](API_StreamInfo.md#KinesisVideo-Type-StreamInfo-KmsKeyId)": "string",
10       "[MediaType](API_StreamInfo.md#KinesisVideo-Type-StreamInfo-MediaType)": "string",
11       "[Status](API_StreamInfo.md#KinesisVideo-Type-StreamInfo-Status)": "string",
12       "[StreamARN](API_StreamInfo.md#KinesisVideo-Type-StreamInfo-StreamARN)": "string",
13       "[StreamName](API_StreamInfo.md#KinesisVideo-Type-StreamInfo-StreamName)": "string",
14       "[Version](API_StreamInfo.md#KinesisVideo-Type-StreamInfo-Version)": "string"
```

```
15    }
16 }
```

Response Elements

If the action is successful, the service sends back an HTTP 200 response.

The following data is returned in JSON format by the service.

** StreamInfo ** An object that describes the stream.
Type: StreamInfo object

Errors

For information about the errors that are common to all actions, see Common Errors.

ClientLimitExceededException
Kinesis Video Streams has throttled the request because you have exceeded the limit of allowed client calls. Try making the call later.
HTTP Status Code: 400

InvalidArgumentException
The value for this input parameter is invalid.
HTTP Status Code: 400

NotAuthorizedException
The caller is not authorized to perform this operation.
HTTP Status Code: 401

ResourceNotFoundException
Amazon Kinesis Video Streams can't find the stream that you specified.
HTTP Status Code: 404

See Also

For more information about using this API in one of the language-specific AWS SDKs, see the following:

- AWS Command Line Interface
- AWS SDK for .NET
- AWS SDK for C++
- AWS SDK for Go
- AWS SDK for Java
- AWS SDK for JavaScript
- AWS SDK for PHP V3
- AWS SDK for Python
- AWS SDK for Ruby V2

GetDataEndpoint

Gets an endpoint for a specified stream for either reading or writing. Use this endpoint in your application to read from the specified stream (using the `GetMedia` or `GetMediaForFragmentList` operations) or write to it (using the `PutMedia` operation).

Note
The returned endpoint does not have the API name appended. The client needs to add the API name to the returned endpoint.

In the request, specify the stream either by `StreamName` or `StreamARN`.

Request Syntax

```
1  POST /getDataEndpoint HTTP/1.1
2  Content-type: application/json
3
4  {
5      "[APIName](#KinesisVideo-GetDataEndpoint-request-APIName)": "string",
6      "[StreamARN](#KinesisVideo-GetDataEndpoint-request-StreamARN)": "string",
7      "[StreamName](#KinesisVideo-GetDataEndpoint-request-StreamName)": "string"
8  }
```

URI Request Parameters

The request does not use any URI parameters.

Request Body

The request accepts the following data in JSON format.

** APIName ** The name of the API action for which to get an endpoint.
Type: String
Valid   Values:PUT_MEDIA | GET_MEDIA | LIST_FRAGMENTS | GET_MEDIA_FOR_FRAGMENT_LIST |
GET_HLS_STREAMING_SESSION_URL
Required: Yes

** StreamARN ** The Amazon Resource Name (ARN) of the stream that you want to get the endpoint for. You must specify either this parameter or a `StreamName` in the request.
Type: String
Length Constraints: Minimum length of 1. Maximum length of 1024.
Pattern: `arn:aws:kinesisvideo:[a-z0-9-]+:[0-9]+:[a-z]+/[a-zA-Z0-9_.-]+/[0-9]+`
Required: No

** StreamName ** The name of the stream that you want to get the endpoint for. You must specify either this parameter or a `StreamARN` in the request.
Type: String
Length Constraints: Minimum length of 1. Maximum length of 256.
Pattern: `[a-zA-Z0-9_.-]+`
Required: No

Response Syntax

```
1 HTTP/1.1 200
2 Content-type: application/json
3
4 {
5   "[DataEndpoint](#KinesisVideo-GetDataEndpoint-response-DataEndpoint)": "string"
6 }
```

Response Elements

If the action is successful, the service sends back an HTTP 200 response.

The following data is returned in JSON format by the service.

** DataEndpoint ** The endpoint value. To read data from the stream or to write data to it, specify this endpoint in your application.
Type: String

Errors

For information about the errors that are common to all actions, see Common Errors.

ClientLimitExceededException
Kinesis Video Streams has throttled the request because you have exceeded the limit of allowed client calls. Try making the call later.
HTTP Status Code: 400

InvalidArgumentException
The value for this input parameter is invalid.
HTTP Status Code: 400

NotAuthorizedException
The caller is not authorized to perform this operation.
HTTP Status Code: 401

ResourceNotFoundException
Amazon Kinesis Video Streams can't find the stream that you specified.
HTTP Status Code: 404

See Also

For more information about using this API in one of the language-specific AWS SDKs, see the following:

- AWS Command Line Interface
- AWS SDK for .NET
- AWS SDK for C++
- AWS SDK for Go
- AWS SDK for Java
- AWS SDK for JavaScript
- AWS SDK for PHP V3
- AWS SDK for Python
- AWS SDK for Ruby V2

ListStreams

Returns an array of `StreamInfo` objects. Each object describes a stream. To retrieve only streams that satisfy a specific condition, you can specify a `StreamNameCondition`.

Request Syntax

```
1 POST /listStreams HTTP/1.1
2 Content-type: application/json
3
4 {
5    "[MaxResults](#KinesisVideo-ListStreams-request-MaxResults)": number,
6    "[NextToken](#KinesisVideo-ListStreams-request-NextToken)": "string",
7    "[StreamNameCondition](#KinesisVideo-ListStreams-request-StreamNameCondition)": {
8        "[ComparisonOperator](API_StreamNameCondition.md#KinesisVideo-Type-StreamNameCondition-
            ComparisonOperator)": "string",
9        "[ComparisonValue](API_StreamNameCondition.md#KinesisVideo-Type-StreamNameCondition-
            ComparisonValue)": "string"
10   }
11 }
```

URI Request Parameters

The request does not use any URI parameters.

Request Body

The request accepts the following data in JSON format.

** MaxResults ** The maximum number of streams to return in the response. The default is 10,000.
Type: Integer
Valid Range: Minimum value of 1. Maximum value of 10000.
Required: No

** NextToken ** If you specify this parameter, when the result of a `ListStreams` operation is truncated, the call returns the `NextToken` in the response. To get another batch of streams, provide this token in your next request.
Type: String
Length Constraints: Minimum length of 0. Maximum length of 512.
Required: No

** StreamNameCondition ** Optional: Returns only streams that satisfy a specific condition. Currently, you can specify only the prefix of a stream name as a condition.
Type: StreamNameCondition object
Required: No

Response Syntax

```
1 HTTP/1.1 200
2 Content-type: application/json
3
4 {
5    "[NextToken](#KinesisVideo-ListStreams-response-NextToken)": "string",
```

```
 6    "[StreamInfoList](#KinesisVideo-ListStreams-response-StreamInfoList)": [
 7        {
 8            "[CreationTime](API_StreamInfo.md#KinesisVideo-Type-StreamInfo-CreationTime)": number,
 9            "[DataRetentionInHours](API_StreamInfo.md#KinesisVideo-Type-StreamInfo-
                  DataRetentionInHours)": number,
10            "[DeviceName](API_StreamInfo.md#KinesisVideo-Type-StreamInfo-DeviceName)": "string",
11            "[KmsKeyId](API_StreamInfo.md#KinesisVideo-Type-StreamInfo-KmsKeyId)": "string",
12            "[MediaType](API_StreamInfo.md#KinesisVideo-Type-StreamInfo-MediaType)": "string",
13            "[Status](API_StreamInfo.md#KinesisVideo-Type-StreamInfo-Status)": "string",
14            "[StreamARN](API_StreamInfo.md#KinesisVideo-Type-StreamInfo-StreamARN)": "string",
15            "[StreamName](API_StreamInfo.md#KinesisVideo-Type-StreamInfo-StreamName)": "string",
16            "[Version](API_StreamInfo.md#KinesisVideo-Type-StreamInfo-Version)": "string"
17        }
18    ]
19 }
```

Response Elements

If the action is successful, the service sends back an HTTP 200 response.

The following data is returned in JSON format by the service.

** NextToken ** If the response is truncated, the call returns this element with a token. To get the next batch of streams, use this token in your next request.
Type: String
Length Constraints: Minimum length of 0. Maximum length of 512.

** StreamInfoList ** An array of `StreamInfo` objects.
Type: Array of StreamInfo objects

Errors

For information about the errors that are common to all actions, see Common Errors.

ClientLimitExceededException
Kinesis Video Streams has throttled the request because you have exceeded the limit of allowed client calls. Try making the call later.
HTTP Status Code: 400

InvalidArgumentException
The value for this input parameter is invalid.
HTTP Status Code: 400

See Also

For more information about using this API in one of the language-specific AWS SDKs, see the following:

- AWS Command Line Interface
- AWS SDK for .NET
- AWS SDK for C++
- AWS SDK for Go
- AWS SDK for Java
- AWS SDK for JavaScript
- AWS SDK for PHP V3
- AWS SDK for Python
- AWS SDK for Ruby V2

ListTagsForStream

Returns a list of tags associated with the specified stream.

In the request, you must specify either the `StreamName` or the `StreamARN`.

Request Syntax

```
1 POST /listTagsForStream HTTP/1.1
2 Content-type: application/json
3
4 {
5    "[NextToken](#KinesisVideo-ListTagsForStream-request-NextToken)": "string",
6    "[StreamARN](#KinesisVideo-ListTagsForStream-request-StreamARN)": "string",
7    "[StreamName](#KinesisVideo-ListTagsForStream-request-StreamName)": "string"
8 }
```

URI Request Parameters

The request does not use any URI parameters.

Request Body

The request accepts the following data in JSON format.

** NextToken ** If you specify this parameter and the result of a `ListTagsForStream` call is truncated, the response includes a token that you can use in the next request to fetch the next batch of tags.
Type: String
Length Constraints: Minimum length of 0. Maximum length of 512.
Required: No

** StreamARN ** The Amazon Resource Name (ARN) of the stream that you want to list tags for.
Type: String
Length Constraints: Minimum length of 1. Maximum length of 1024.
Pattern: `arn:aws:kinesisvideo:[a-z0-9-]+:[0-9]+:[a-z]+/[a-zA-Z0-9_.-]+/[0-9]+`
Required: No

** StreamName ** The name of the stream that you want to list tags for.
Type: String
Length Constraints: Minimum length of 1. Maximum length of 256.
Pattern: `[a-zA-Z0-9_.-]+`
Required: No

Response Syntax

```
1 HTTP/1.1 200
2 Content-type: application/json
3
4 {
5    "[NextToken](#KinesisVideo-ListTagsForStream-response-NextToken)": "string",
6    "[Tags](#KinesisVideo-ListTagsForStream-response-Tags)": {
7       "string" : "string"
8    }
```

```
9 }
```

Response Elements

If the action is successful, the service sends back an HTTP 200 response.

The following data is returned in JSON format by the service.

** NextToken ** If you specify this parameter and the result of a `ListTags` call is truncated, the response includes a token that you can use in the next request to fetch the next set of tags.
Type: String
Length Constraints: Minimum length of 0. Maximum length of 512.

** Tags ** A map of tag keys and values associated with the specified stream.
Type: String to string map
Key Length Constraints: Minimum length of 1. Maximum length of 128.
Value Length Constraints: Minimum length of 0. Maximum length of 256.

Errors

For information about the errors that are common to all actions, see Common Errors.

ClientLimitExceededException
Kinesis Video Streams has throttled the request because you have exceeded the limit of allowed client calls. Try making the call later.
HTTP Status Code: 400

InvalidArgumentException
The value for this input parameter is invalid.
HTTP Status Code: 400

InvalidResourceFormatException
The format of the `StreamARN` is invalid.
HTTP Status Code: 400

NotAuthorizedException
The caller is not authorized to perform this operation.
HTTP Status Code: 401

ResourceNotFoundException
Amazon Kinesis Video Streams can't find the stream that you specified.
HTTP Status Code: 404

See Also

For more information about using this API in one of the language-specific AWS SDKs, see the following:

- AWS Command Line Interface
- AWS SDK for .NET
- AWS SDK for C++
- AWS SDK for Go
- AWS SDK for Java
- AWS SDK for JavaScript
- AWS SDK for PHP V3
- AWS SDK for Python
- AWS SDK for Ruby V2

TagStream

Adds one or more tags to a stream. A *tag* is a key-value pair (the value is optional) that you can define and assign to AWS resources. If you specify a tag that already exists, the tag value is replaced with the value that you specify in the request. For more information, see Using Cost Allocation Tags in the *AWS Billing and Cost Management User Guide*.

You must provide either the `StreamName` or the `StreamARN`.

This operation requires permission for the `KinesisVideo:TagStream` action.

Kinesis video streams support up to 50 tags.

Request Syntax

```
1  POST /tagStream HTTP/1.1
2  Content-type: application/json
3
4  {
5     "[StreamARN](#KinesisVideo-TagStream-request-StreamARN)": "string",
6     "[StreamName](#KinesisVideo-TagStream-request-StreamName)": "string",
7     "[Tags](#KinesisVideo-TagStream-request-Tags)": {
8        "string" : "string"
9     }
10 }
```

URI Request Parameters

The request does not use any URI parameters.

Request Body

The request accepts the following data in JSON format.

** StreamARN ** The Amazon Resource Name (ARN) of the resource that you want to add the tag or tags to.
Type: String
Length Constraints: Minimum length of 1. Maximum length of 1024.
Pattern: `arn:aws:kinesisvideo:[a-z0-9-]+:[0-9]+:[a-z]+/[a-zA-Z0-9_.-]+/[0-9]+`
Required: No

** StreamName ** The name of the stream that you want to add the tag or tags to.
Type: String
Length Constraints: Minimum length of 1. Maximum length of 256.
Pattern: `[a-zA-Z0-9_.-]+`
Required: No

** Tags ** A list of tags to associate with the specified stream. Each tag is a key-value pair (the value is optional).
Type: String to string map
Key Length Constraints: Minimum length of 1. Maximum length of 128.
Value Length Constraints: Minimum length of 0. Maximum length of 256.
Required: Yes

Response Syntax

```
1 HTTP/1.1 200
```

Response Elements

If the action is successful, the service sends back an HTTP 200 response with an empty HTTP body.

Errors

For information about the errors that are common to all actions, see Common Errors.

ClientLimitExceededException
Kinesis Video Streams has throttled the request because you have exceeded the limit of allowed client calls. Try making the call later.
HTTP Status Code: 400

InvalidArgumentException
The value for this input parameter is invalid.
HTTP Status Code: 400

InvalidResourceFormatException
The format of the `StreamARN` is invalid.
HTTP Status Code: 400

NotAuthorizedException
The caller is not authorized to perform this operation.
HTTP Status Code: 401

ResourceNotFoundException
Amazon Kinesis Video Streams can't find the stream that you specified.
HTTP Status Code: 404

TagsPerResourceExceededLimitException
You have exceeded the limit of tags that you can associate with the resource. Kinesis video streams support up to 50 tags.
HTTP Status Code: 400

See Also

For more information about using this API in one of the language-specific AWS SDKs, see the following:

- AWS Command Line Interface
- AWS SDK for .NET
- AWS SDK for C++
- AWS SDK for Go
- AWS SDK for Java
- AWS SDK for JavaScript
- AWS SDK for PHP V3
- AWS SDK for Python
- AWS SDK for Ruby V2

UntagStream

Removes one or more tags from a stream. In the request, specify only a tag key or keys; don't specify the value. If you specify a tag key that does not exist, it's ignored.

In the request, you must provide the `StreamName` or `StreamARN`.

Request Syntax

```
1 POST /untagStream HTTP/1.1
2 Content-type: application/json
3
4 {
5    "[StreamARN](#KinesisVideo-UntagStream-request-StreamARN)": "string",
6    "[StreamName](#KinesisVideo-UntagStream-request-StreamName)": "string",
7    "[TagKeyList](#KinesisVideo-UntagStream-request-TagKeyList)": [ "string" ]
8 }
```

URI Request Parameters

The request does not use any URI parameters.

Request Body

The request accepts the following data in JSON format.

** StreamARN ** The Amazon Resource Name (ARN) of the stream that you want to remove tags from.
Type: String
Length Constraints: Minimum length of 1. Maximum length of 1024.
Pattern: `arn:aws:kinesisvideo:[a-z0-9-]+:[0-9]+:[a-z]+/[a-zA-Z0-9_.-]+/[0-9]+`
Required: No

** StreamName ** The name of the stream that you want to remove tags from.
Type: String
Length Constraints: Minimum length of 1. Maximum length of 256.
Pattern: `[a-zA-Z0-9_.-]+`
Required: No

** TagKeyList ** A list of the keys of the tags that you want to remove.
Type: Array of strings
Array Members: Minimum number of 1 item. Maximum number of 50 items.
Length Constraints: Minimum length of 1. Maximum length of 128.
Required: Yes

Response Syntax

```
1 HTTP/1.1 200
```

Response Elements

If the action is successful, the service sends back an HTTP 200 response with an empty HTTP body.

Errors

For information about the errors that are common to all actions, see Common Errors.

ClientLimitExceededException
Kinesis Video Streams has throttled the request because you have exceeded the limit of allowed client calls. Try making the call later.
HTTP Status Code: 400

InvalidArgumentException
The value for this input parameter is invalid.
HTTP Status Code: 400

InvalidResourceFormatException
The format of the `StreamARN` is invalid.
HTTP Status Code: 400

NotAuthorizedException
The caller is not authorized to perform this operation.
HTTP Status Code: 401

ResourceNotFoundException
Amazon Kinesis Video Streams can't find the stream that you specified.
HTTP Status Code: 404

See Also

For more information about using this API in one of the language-specific AWS SDKs, see the following:

- AWS Command Line Interface
- AWS SDK for .NET
- AWS SDK for C++
- AWS SDK for Go
- AWS SDK for Java
- AWS SDK for JavaScript
- AWS SDK for PHP V3
- AWS SDK for Python
- AWS SDK for Ruby V2

UpdateDataRetention

Increases or decreases the stream's data retention period by the value that you specify. To indicate whether you want to increase or decrease the data retention period, specify the `Operation` parameter in the request body. In the request, you must specify either the `StreamName` or the `StreamARN`.

Note
The retention period that you specify replaces the current value.

This operation requires permission for the `KinesisVideo:UpdateDataRetention` action.

Changing the data retention period affects the data in the stream as follows:

- If the data retention period is increased, existing data is retained for the new retention period. For example, if the data retention period is increased from one hour to seven hours, all existing data is retained for seven hours.
- If the data retention period is decreased, existing data is retained for the new retention period. For example, if the data retention period is decreased from seven hours to one hour, all existing data is retained for one hour, and any data older than one hour is deleted immediately.

Request Syntax

```
1 POST /updateDataRetention HTTP/1.1
2 Content-type: application/json
3
4 {
5    "[CurrentVersion](#KinesisVideo-UpdateDataRetention-request-CurrentVersion)": "string",
6    "[DataRetentionChangeInHours](#KinesisVideo-UpdateDataRetention-request-
          DataRetentionChangeInHours)": number,
7    "[Operation](#KinesisVideo-UpdateDataRetention-request-Operation)": "string",
8    "[StreamARN](#KinesisVideo-UpdateDataRetention-request-StreamARN)": "string",
9    "[StreamName](#KinesisVideo-UpdateDataRetention-request-StreamName)": "string"
10 }
```

URI Request Parameters

The request does not use any URI parameters.

Request Body

The request accepts the following data in JSON format.

** CurrentVersion ** The version of the stream whose retention period you want to change. To get the version, call either the `DescribeStream` or the `ListStreams` API.
Type: String
Length Constraints: Minimum length of 1. Maximum length of 64.
Pattern: `[a-zA-Z0-9]+`
Required: Yes

** DataRetentionChangeInHours ** The retention period, in hours. The value you specify replaces the current value.
Type: Integer
Valid Range: Minimum value of 1.
Required: Yes

** Operation ** Indicates whether you want to increase or decrease the retention period.
Type: String
Valid Values:`INCREASE_DATA_RETENTION` | `DECREASE_DATA_RETENTION`
Required: Yes

** StreamARN ** The Amazon Resource Name (ARN) of the stream whose retention period you want to change.
Type: String
Length Constraints: Minimum length of 1. Maximum length of 1024.
Pattern: `arn:aws:kinesisvideo:[a-z0-9-]+:[0-9]+:[a-z]+/[a-zA-Z0-9_.-]+/[0-9]+`
Required: No

** StreamName ** The name of the stream whose retention period you want to change.
Type: String
Length Constraints: Minimum length of 1. Maximum length of 256.
Pattern: `[a-zA-Z0-9_.-]+`
Required: No

Response Syntax

```
1 HTTP/1.1 200
```

Response Elements

If the action is successful, the service sends back an HTTP 200 response with an empty HTTP body.

Errors

For information about the errors that are common to all actions, see Common Errors.

ClientLimitExceededException
Kinesis Video Streams has throttled the request because you have exceeded the limit of allowed client calls. Try making the call later.
HTTP Status Code: 400

InvalidArgumentException
The value for this input parameter is invalid.
HTTP Status Code: 400

NotAuthorizedException
The caller is not authorized to perform this operation.
HTTP Status Code: 401

ResourceInUseException
The stream is currently not available for this operation.
HTTP Status Code: 400

ResourceNotFoundException
Amazon Kinesis Video Streams can't find the stream that you specified.
HTTP Status Code: 404

VersionMismatchException
The stream version that you specified is not the latest version. To get the latest version, use the DescribeStream API.
HTTP Status Code: 400

See Also

For more information about using this API in one of the language-specific AWS SDKs, see the following:

- AWS Command Line Interface
- AWS SDK for .NET
- AWS SDK for C++
- AWS SDK for Go
- AWS SDK for Java
- AWS SDK for JavaScript
- AWS SDK for PHP V3
- AWS SDK for Python
- AWS SDK for Ruby V2

UpdateStream

Updates stream metadata, such as the device name and media type.

You must provide the stream name or the Amazon Resource Name (ARN) of the stream.

To make sure that you have the latest version of the stream before updating it, you can specify the stream version. Kinesis Video Streams assigns a version to each stream. When you update a stream, Kinesis Video Streams assigns a new version number. To get the latest stream version, use the `DescribeStream` API.

`UpdateStream` is an asynchronous operation, and takes time to complete.

Request Syntax

```
1  POST /updateStream HTTP/1.1
2  Content-type: application/json
3
4  {
5     "[CurrentVersion](#KinesisVideo-UpdateStream-request-CurrentVersion)": "string",
6     "[DeviceName](#KinesisVideo-UpdateStream-request-DeviceName)": "string",
7     "[MediaType](#KinesisVideo-UpdateStream-request-MediaType)": "string",
8     "[StreamARN](#KinesisVideo-UpdateStream-request-StreamARN)": "string",
9     "[StreamName](#KinesisVideo-UpdateStream-request-StreamName)": "string"
10 }
```

URI Request Parameters

The request does not use any URI parameters.

Request Body

The request accepts the following data in JSON format.

** CurrentVersion ** The version of the stream whose metadata you want to update.
Type: String
Length Constraints: Minimum length of 1. Maximum length of 64.
Pattern: `[a-zA-Z0-9]+`
Required: Yes

** DeviceName ** The name of the device that is writing to the stream.
In the current implementation, Kinesis Video Streams does not use this name. Type: String
Length Constraints: Minimum length of 1. Maximum length of 128.
Pattern: `[a-zA-Z0-9_.-]+`
Required: No

** MediaType ** The stream's media type. Use `MediaType` to specify the type of content that the stream contains to the consumers of the stream. For more information about media types, see Media Types. If you choose to specify the `MediaType`, see Naming Requirements.
To play video on the console, you must specify the correct video type. For example, if the video in the stream is H.264, specify `video/h264` as the `MediaType`.
Type: String
Length Constraints: Minimum length of 1. Maximum length of 128.
Pattern: `[\w\-\.\+]+/[\w\-\.\+]+`
Required: No

171

** StreamARN ** The ARN of the stream whose metadata you want to update.
Type: String
Length Constraints: Minimum length of 1. Maximum length of 1024.
Pattern: `arn:aws:kinesisvideo:[a-z0-9-]+:[0-9]+:[a-z]+/[a-zA-Z0-9_.-]+/[0-9]+`
Required: No

** StreamName ** The name of the stream whose metadata you want to update.
The stream name is an identifier for the stream, and must be unique for each account and region.
Type: String
Length Constraints: Minimum length of 1. Maximum length of 256.
Pattern: `[a-zA-Z0-9_.-]+`
Required: No

Response Syntax

```
1 HTTP/1.1 200
```

Response Elements

If the action is successful, the service sends back an HTTP 200 response with an empty HTTP body.

Errors

For information about the errors that are common to all actions, see Common Errors.

ClientLimitExceededException
Kinesis Video Streams has throttled the request because you have exceeded the limit of allowed client calls. Try making the call later.
HTTP Status Code: 400

InvalidArgumentException
The value for this input parameter is invalid.
HTTP Status Code: 400

NotAuthorizedException
The caller is not authorized to perform this operation.
HTTP Status Code: 401

ResourceInUseException
The stream is currently not available for this operation.
HTTP Status Code: 400

ResourceNotFoundException
Amazon Kinesis Video Streams can't find the stream that you specified.
HTTP Status Code: 404

VersionMismatchException
The stream version that you specified is not the latest version. To get the latest version, use the DescribeStream API.
HTTP Status Code: 400

See Also

For more information about using this API in one of the language-specific AWS SDKs, see the following:

- AWS Command Line Interface

- AWS SDK for .NET
- AWS SDK for C++
- AWS SDK for Go
- AWS SDK for Java
- AWS SDK for JavaScript
- AWS SDK for PHP V3
- AWS SDK for Python
- AWS SDK for Ruby V2

Amazon Kinesis Video Streams Media

The following data types are supported by Amazon Kinesis Video Streams Media:

- StartSelector

GetMedia

Use this API to retrieve media content from a Kinesis video stream. In the request, you identify the stream name or stream Amazon Resource Name (ARN), and the starting chunk. Kinesis Video Streams then returns a stream of chunks in order by fragment number.

Note
You must first call the `GetDataEndpoint` API to get an endpoint. Then send the `GetMedia` requests to this endpoint using the --endpoint-url parameter.

When you put media data (fragments) on a stream, Kinesis Video Streams stores each incoming fragment and related metadata in what is called a "chunk." For more information, see PutMedia. The `GetMedia` API returns a stream of these chunks starting from the chunk that you specify in the request.

The following limits apply when using the `GetMedia` API:

- A client can call `GetMedia` up to five times per second per stream.
- Kinesis Video Streams sends media data at a rate of up to 25 megabytes per second (or 200 megabits per second) during a `GetMedia` session.

Request Syntax

```
1  POST /getMedia HTTP/1.1
2  Content-type: application/json
3
4  {
5     "[StartSelector](#KinesisVideo-dataplane_GetMedia-request-StartSelector)": {
6        "[AfterFragmentNumber](API_dataplane_StartSelector.md#KinesisVideo-Type-
            dataplane_StartSelector-AfterFragmentNumber)": "string",
7        "[ContinuationToken](API_dataplane_StartSelector.md#KinesisVideo-Type-
            dataplane_StartSelector-ContinuationToken)": "string",
8        "[StartSelectorType](API_dataplane_StartSelector.md#KinesisVideo-Type-
            dataplane_StartSelector-StartSelectorType)": "string",
9        "[StartTimestamp](API_dataplane_StartSelector.md#KinesisVideo-Type-dataplane_StartSelector
            -StartTimestamp)": number
10    },
11    "[StreamARN](#KinesisVideo-dataplane_GetMedia-request-StreamARN)": "string",
12    "[StreamName](#KinesisVideo-dataplane_GetMedia-request-StreamName)": "string"
13 }
```

URI Request Parameters

The request does not use any URI parameters.

Request Body

The request accepts the following data in JSON format.

** StartSelector ** Identifies the starting chunk to get from the specified stream.
Type: StartSelector object
Required: Yes

** StreamARN ** The ARN of the stream from where you want to get the media content. If you don't specify the `streamARN`, you must specify the `streamName`.
Type: String

Length Constraints: Minimum length of 1. Maximum length of 1024.

Pattern: `arn:aws:kinesisvideo:[a-z0-9-]+:[0-9]+:[a-z]+/[a-zA-Z0-9_.-]+/[0-9]+`

Required: No

** StreamName ** The Kinesis video stream name from where you want to get the media content. If you don't specify the `streamName`, you must specify the `streamARN`.

Type: String

Length Constraints: Minimum length of 1. Maximum length of 256.

Pattern: `[a-zA-Z0-9_.-]+`

Required: No

Response Syntax

```
1 HTTP/1.1 200
2 Content-Type: ContentType
3
4 Payload
```

Response Elements

If the action is successful, the service sends back an HTTP 200 response.

The response returns the following HTTP headers.

** ContentType ** The content type of the requested media.

Length Constraints: Minimum length of 1. Maximum length of 128.

Pattern: `^[a-zA-Z0-9_\.\-]+$`

The response returns the following as the HTTP body.

** Payload ** The payload Kinesis Video Streams returns is a sequence of chunks from the specified stream. For information about the chunks, see PutMedia. The chunks that Kinesis Video Streams returns in the `GetMedia` call also include the following additional Matroska (MKV) tags:

- AWS_KINESISVIDEO_CONTINUATION_TOKEN (UTF-8 string) - In the event your `GetMedia` call terminates, you can use this continuation token in your next request to get the next chunk where the last request terminated.
- AWS_KINESISVIDEO_MILLIS_BEHIND_NOW (UTF-8 string) - Client applications can use this tag value to determine how far behind the chunk returned in the response is from the latest chunk on the stream.
- AWS_KINESISVIDEO_FRAGMENT_NUMBER - Fragment number returned in the chunk.
- AWS_KINESISVIDEO_SERVER_TIMESTAMP - Server time stamp of the fragment.
- AWS_KINESISVIDEO_PRODUCER_TIMESTAMP - Producer time stamp of the fragment. The following tags will be present if an error occurs:
- AWS_KINESISVIDEO_ERROR_CODE - String description of an error that caused GetMedia to stop.
- AWS_KINESISVIDEO_ERROR_ID: Integer code of the error. The error codes are as follows:
- 3002 - Error writing to the stream
- 4000 - Requested fragment is not found
- 4500 - Access denied for the stream's KMS key
- 4501 - Stream's KMS key is disabled
- 4502 - Validation error on the Stream's KMS key
- 4503 - KMS key specified in the stream is unavailable
- 4504 - Invalid usage of the KMS key specified in the stream
- 4505 - Invalid state of the KMS key specified in the stream
- 4506 - Unable to find the KMS key specified in the stream
- 5000 - Internal error

Errors

For information about the errors that are common to all actions, see Common Errors.

ClientLimitExceededException
Kinesis Video Streams has throttled the request because you have exceeded the limit of allowed client calls. Try making the call later.
HTTP Status Code: 400

ConnectionLimitExceededException
Kinesis Video Streams has throttled the request because you have exceeded the limit of allowed client connections.
HTTP Status Code: 400

InvalidArgumentException
The value for this input parameter is invalid.
HTTP Status Code: 400

InvalidEndpointException
Status Code: 400, Caller used wrong endpoint to write data to a stream. On receiving such an exception, the user must call `GetDataEndpoint` with `AccessMode` set to "READ" and use the endpoint Kinesis Video returns in the next `GetMedia` call.
HTTP Status Code: 400

NotAuthorizedException
Status Code: 403, The caller is not authorized to perform an operation on the given stream, or the token has expired.
HTTP Status Code: 401

ResourceNotFoundException
Status Code: 404, The stream with the given name does not exist.
HTTP Status Code: 404

See Also

For more information about using this API in one of the language-specific AWS SDKs, see the following:

- AWS Command Line Interface
- AWS SDK for .NET
- AWS SDK for C++
- AWS SDK for Go
- AWS SDK for Java
- AWS SDK for JavaScript
- AWS SDK for PHP V3
- AWS SDK for Python
- AWS SDK for Ruby V2

PutMedia

Use this API to send media data to a Kinesis video stream.

Note
Before using this API, you must call the `GetDataEndpoint` API to get an endpoint. You then specify the endpoint in your `PutMedia` request.

In the request, you use the HTTP headers to provide parameter information, for example, stream name, time stamp, and whether the time stamp value is absolute or relative to when the producer started recording. You use the request body to send the media data. Kinesis Video Streams supports only the Matroska (MKV) container format for sending media data using this API.

You have the following options for sending data using this API:

- Send media data in real time: For example, a security camera can send frames in real time as it generates them. This approach minimizes the latency between the video recording and data sent on the wire. This is referred to as a continuous producer. In this case, a consumer application can read the stream in real time or when needed.
- Send media data offline (in batches): For example, a body camera might record video for hours and store it on the device. Later, when you connect the camera to the docking port, the camera can start a `PutMedia` session to send data to a Kinesis video stream. In this scenario, latency is not an issue.

When using this API, note the following considerations:

- You must specify either `streamName` or `streamARN`, but not both.
- You might find it easier to use a single long-running `PutMedia` session and send a large number of media data fragments in the payload. Note that for each fragment received, Kinesis Video Streams sends one or more acknowledgements. Potential network considerations might cause you to not get all these acknowledgements as they are generated.
- You might choose multiple consecutive `PutMedia` sessions, each with fewer fragments to ensure that you get all acknowledgements from the service in real time.

Note
If you send data to the same stream on multiple simultaneous `PutMedia` sessions, the media fragments get interleaved on the stream. You should make sure that this is OK in your application scenario.

The following limits apply when using the `PutMedia` API:

- A client can call `PutMedia` up to five times per second per stream.
- A client can send up to five fragments per second per stream.
- Kinesis Video Streams reads media data at a rate of up to 12.5 MB/second, or 100 Mbps during a `PutMedia` session.

Note the following constraints. In these cases, Kinesis Video Streams sends the Error acknowledgement in the response.

- Fragments that have time codes spanning longer than 10 seconds and that contain more than 50 megabytes of data are not allowed.
- An MKV stream containing more than one MKV segment or containing disallowed MKV elements (like `track*`) also results in the Error acknowledgement.

Kinesis Video Streams stores each incoming fragment and related metadata in what is called a "chunk." The fragment metadata includes the following:

- The MKV headers provided at the start of the `PutMedia` request

- The following Kinesis Video Streams-specific metadata for the fragment:

  - `server_timestamp` - Time stamp when Kinesis Video Streams started receiving the fragment.

- producer_timestamp - Time stamp, when the producer started recording the fragment. Kinesis Video Streams uses three pieces of information received in the request to calculate this value.
- The fragment timecode value received in the request body along with the fragment.
- Two request headers: producerStartTimestamp (when the producer started recording) and fragmentTimeCodeType (whether the fragment timecode in the payload is absolute or relative).

Kinesis Video Streams then computes the producer_timestamp for the fragment as follows:

If fragmentTimeCodeType is relative, then

producer_timestamp = producerStartTimeStamp + fragment timecode

If fragmentTimeCodeType is absolute, then

producer_timestamp = fragment timecode (converted to milliseconds)

- Unique fragment number assigned by Kinesis Video Streams.

Note
When you make the GetMedia request, Kinesis Video Streams returns a stream of these chunks. The client can process the metadata as needed.

Note
This operation is only available for the AWS SDK for Java. It is not supported in AWS SDKs for other languages.

Request Syntax

```
1 POST /putMedia HTTP/1.1
2 x-amzn-stream-name: StreamName
3 x-amzn-stream-arn: StreamARN
4 x-amzn-fragment-timecode-type: FragmentTimecodeType
5 x-amzn-producer-start-timestamp: ProducerStartTimestamp
6
7 Payload
```

URI Request Parameters

The request requires the following URI parameters.

** FragmentTimecodeType ** You pass this value as the x-amzn-fragment-timecode-type HTTP header. Indicates whether timecodes in the fragments (payload, HTTP request body) are absolute or relative to producerStartTimestamp. Kinesis Video Streams uses this information to compute the producer_timestamp for the fragment received in the request, as described in the API overview.
Valid Values:ABSOLUTE | RELATIVE

** ProducerStartTimestamp ** You pass this value as the x-amzn-producer-start-timestamp HTTP header. This is the producer time stamp at which the producer started recording the media (not the time stamp of the specific fragments in the request).

** StreamARN ** You pass this value as the x-amzn-stream-arn HTTP header.
Amazon Resource Name (ARN) of the Kinesis video stream where you want to write the media content. If you don't specify the streamARN, you must specify the streamName.
Length Constraints: Minimum length of 1. Maximum length of 1024.
Pattern: arn:aws:kinesisvideo:[a-z0-9-]+:[0-9]+:[a-z]+/[a-zA-Z0-9_.-]+/[0-9]+

** StreamName ** You pass this value as the x-amzn-stream-name HTTP header.
Name of the Kinesis video stream where you want to write the media content. If you don't specify the streamName, you must specify the streamARN.
Length Constraints: Minimum length of 1. Maximum length of 256.
Pattern: [a-zA-Z0-9_.-]+

Request Body

The request accepts the following binary data.

** Payload ** The media content to write to the Kinesis video stream. In the current implementation, Kinesis Video Streams supports only the Matroska (MKV) container format with a single MKV segment. A segment can contain one or more clusters.
Each MKV cluster maps to a Kinesis video stream fragment. Whatever cluster duration you choose becomes the fragment duration.

Response Syntax

```
1 HTTP/1.1 200
2
3 Payload
```

Response Elements

If the action is successful, the service sends back an HTTP 200 response.

The response returns the following as the HTTP body.

** Payload ** After Kinesis Video Streams successfully receives a `PutMedia` request, the service validates the request headers. The service then starts reading the payload and first sends an HTTP 200 response.
The service then returns a stream containing a series of JSON objects (`Acknowledgement` objects) separated by newlines. The acknowledgements are received on the same connection on which the media data is sent. There can be many acknowledgements for a `PutMedia` request. Each `Acknowledgement` consists of the following key-value pairs:

- `AckEventType` - Event type the acknowledgement represents.
- **Buffering:** Kinesis Video Streams has started receiving the fragment. Kinesis Video Streams sends the first Buffering acknowledgement when the first byte of fragment data is received.
- **Received:** Kinesis Video Streams received the entire fragment. If you did not configure the stream to persist the data, the producer can stop buffering the fragment upon receiving this acknowledgement.
- **Persisted:** Kinesis Video Streams has persisted the fragment (for example, to Amazon S3). You get this acknowledgement if you configured the stream to persist the data. After you receive this acknowledgement, the producer can stop buffering the fragment.
- **Error:** Kinesis Video Streams ran into an error while processing the fragment. You can review the error code and determine the next course of action.
- **Idle:** The `PutMedia` session is in-progress. However, Kinesis Video Streams is currently not receiving data. Kinesis Video Streams sends this acknowledgement periodically for up to 30 seconds after the last received data. If no data is received within the 30 seconds, Kinesis Video Streams closes the request. **Note** This acknowledgement can help a producer determine if the `PutMedia` connection is alive, even if it is not sending any data.
- `FragmentTimeCode` - Fragment timecode for which acknowledgement is sent.

The element can be missing if the `AckEventType` is **Idle**.

- `FragmentNumber` - Kinesis Video Streams-generated fragment number for which the acknowledgement is sent.
- `ErrorId` and `ErrorCode` - If the `AckEventType` is ErrorId, this field provides corresponding error code. The following is the list of error codes:
- 4000 - Error reading the data stream.
- 4001 - Fragment size is greater than maximum limit, 50 MB, allowed.
- 4002 - Fragment duration is greater than maximum limit, 10 seconds, allowed.
- 4003 - Connection duration is greater than maximum allowed threshold.

- 4004 - Fragment timecode is less than the timecode previous time code (within a `PutMedia` call, you cannot send fragments out of order).
- 4005 - More than one track is found in MKV.
- 4006 - Failed to parse the input stream as valid MKV format.
- 4007 - Invalid producer timestamp.
- 4008 - Stream no longer exists (deleted).
- 4500 - Access to the stream's specified KMS key is denied.
- 4501 - The stream's specified KMS key is disabled.
- 4502 - The stream's specified KMS key failed validation.
- 4503 - The stream's specified KMS key is unavailable.
- 4504 - Invalid usage of the stream's specified KMS key.
- 4505 - The stream's specified KMS key is in an invalid state.
- 4506 - The stream's specified KMS key is not found.
- 5000 - Internal service error
- 5001 - Kinesis Video Streams failed to persist fragments to the data store. The producer, while sending the payload for a long running `PutMedia` request, should read the response for acknowledgements. A producer might receive chunks of acknowledgements at the same time, due to buffering on an intermediate proxy server. A producer that wants to receive timely acknowledgements can send fewer fragments in each `PutMedia` request.

Errors

For information about the errors that are common to all actions, see Common Errors.

ClientLimitExceededException
Kinesis Video Streams has throttled the request because you have exceeded the limit of allowed client calls. Try making the call later.
HTTP Status Code: 400

ConnectionLimitExceededException
Kinesis Video Streams has throttled the request because you have exceeded the limit of allowed client connections.
HTTP Status Code: 400

InvalidArgumentException
The value for this input parameter is invalid.
HTTP Status Code: 400

InvalidEndpointException
Status Code: 400, Caller used wrong endpoint to write data to a stream. On receiving such an exception, the user must call `GetDataEndpoint` with `AccessMode` set to "READ" and use the endpoint Kinesis Video returns in the next `GetMedia` call.
HTTP Status Code: 400

NotAuthorizedException
Status Code: 403, The caller is not authorized to perform an operation on the given stream, or the token has expired.
HTTP Status Code: 401

ResourceNotFoundException
Status Code: 404, The stream with the given name does not exist.
HTTP Status Code: 404

Example

Acknowledgement Format

The format of the acknowledgement is as follows:

```
{
    Acknowledgement : {""
        EventType: enum
        "FragmentTimecode": Long,""
        FragmentNumber: Long,""
        ErrorId : String
    }
}
```

See Also

For more information about using this API in one of the language-specific AWS SDKs, see the following:

- AWS Command Line Interface
- AWS SDK for .NET
- AWS SDK for C++
- AWS SDK for Go
- AWS SDK for Java
- AWS SDK for JavaScript
- AWS SDK for PHP V3
- AWS SDK for Python
- AWS SDK for Ruby V2

Amazon Kinesis Video Streams Archived Media

The following data types are supported by Amazon Kinesis Video Streams Archived Media:

- Fragment
- FragmentSelector
- HLSFragmentSelector
- HLSTimestampRange
- TimestampRange

GetHLSStreamingSessionURL

Retrieves an HTTP Live Streaming (HLS) URL for the stream. The URL can then be opened in a browser or media player to view the stream contents.

You must specify either the `StreamName` or the `StreamARN`.

An Amazon Kinesis video stream has the following requirements for providing data through HLS:

- The media type must be `video/h264`.
- Data retention must be greater than 0.
- The fragments must contain codec private data in the AVC (Advanced Video Coding) for H.264 format (MPEG-4 specification ISO/IEC 14496-15). For information about adapting stream data to a given format, see NAL Adaptation Flags.

Kinesis Video Streams HLS sessions contain fragments in the fragmented MPEG-4 form (also called fMP4 or CMAF), rather than the MPEG-2 form (also called TS chunks, which the HLS specification also supports). For more information about HLS fragment types, see the HLS specification.

The following procedure shows how to use HLS with Kinesis Video Streams:

1. Get an endpoint using GetDataEndpoint, specifying `GET_HLS_STREAMING_SESSION_URL` for the `APIName` parameter.

2. Retrieve the HLS URL using `GetHLSStreamingSessionURL`. Kinesis Video Streams creates an HLS streaming session to be used for accessing content in a stream using the HLS protocol. `GetHLSStreamingSessionURL` returns an authenticated URL (that includes an encrypted session token) for the session's HLS *master playlist* (the root resource needed for streaming with HLS). **Note** Don't share or store this token where an unauthorized entity could access it. The token provides access to the content of the stream. Safeguard the token with the same measures that you would use with your AWS credentials.

   The media that is made available through the playlist consists only of the requested stream, time range, and format. No other media data (such as frames outside the requested window or alternate bit rates) is made available.

3. Provide the URL (containing the encrypted session token) for the HLS master playlist to a media player that supports the HLS protocol. Kinesis Video Streams makes the HLS media playlist, initialization fragment, and media fragments available through the master playlist URL. The initialization fragment contains the codec private data for the stream, and other data needed to set up the video decoder and renderer. The media fragments contain H.264-encoded video frames and time stamps.

4. The media player receives the authenticated URL and requests stream metadata and media data normally. When the media player requests data, it calls the following actions:

   - **GetHLSMasterPlaylist:** Retrieves an HLS master playlist, which contains a URL for the `GetHLSMediaPlaylist` action, and additional metadata for the media player, including estimated bit rate and resolution.
   - **GetHLSMediaPlaylist:** Retrieves an HLS media playlist, which contains a URL to access the MP4 intitialization fragment with the `GetMP4InitFragment` action, and URLs to access the MP4 media fragments with the `GetMP4MediaFragment` actions. The HLS media playlist also contains metadata about the stream that the player needs to play it, such as whether the `PlaybackMode` is `LIVE` or `ON_DEMAND`. The HLS media playlist is typically static for sessions with a `PlaybackType` of `ON_DEMAND`. The HLS media playlist is continually updated with new fragments for sessions with a `PlaybackType` of `LIVE`.
   - **GetMP4InitFragment:** Retrieves the MP4 initialization fragment. The media player typically loads the initialization fragment before loading any media fragments. This fragment contains the "fytp" and "moov" MP4 atoms, and the child atoms that are needed to initialize the media player decoder.

The initialization fragment does not correspond to a fragment in a Kinesis video stream. It contains only the codec private data for the stream, which the media player needs to decode video frames.

- **GetMP4MediaFragment:** Retrieves MP4 media fragments. These fragments contain the "moof" and "mdat" MP4 atoms and their child atoms, containing the encoded fragment's video frames and their time stamps. **Note**
  After the first media fragment is made available in a streaming session, any fragments that don't contain the same codec private data are excluded in the HLS media playlist. Therefore, the codec private data does not change between fragments in a session.

Note

The following restrictions apply to HLS sessions:
A streaming session URL should not be shared between players. The service might throttle a session if multiple media players are sharing it. For connection limits, see Kinesis Video Streams Limits. A Kinesis video stream can have a maximum of five active HLS streaming sessions. If a new session is created when the maximum number of sessions is already active, the oldest (earliest created) session is closed. The number of active `GetMedia` connections on a Kinesis video stream does not count against this limit, and the number of active HLS sessions does not count against the active `GetMedia` connection limit.

You can monitor the amount of data that the media player consumes by monitoring the `GetMP4MediaFragment` `.OutgoingBytes` Amazon CloudWatch metric. For information about using CloudWatch to monitor Kinesis Video Streams, see Monitoring Kinesis Video Streams. For pricing information, see Amazon Kinesis Video Streams Pricing and AWS Pricing. Charges for both HLS sessions and outgoing AWS data apply.

For more information about HLS, see HTTP Live Streaming on the Apple Developer site.

Request Syntax

```
1  POST /getHLSStreamingSessionURL HTTP/1.1
2  Content-type: application/json
3
4  {
5     "[DiscontinuityMode](#KinesisVideo-reader_GetHLSStreamingSessionURL-request-DiscontinuityMode
          )": "string",
6     "[Expires](#KinesisVideo-reader_GetHLSStreamingSessionURL-request-Expires)": number,
7     "[HLSFragmentSelector](#KinesisVideo-reader_GetHLSStreamingSessionURL-request-
          HLSFragmentSelector)": {
8        "[FragmentSelectorType](API_reader_HLSFragmentSelector.md#KinesisVideo-Type-
             reader_HLSFragmentSelector-FragmentSelectorType)": "string",
9        "[TimestampRange](API_reader_HLSFragmentSelector.md#KinesisVideo-Type-
             reader_HLSFragmentSelector-TimestampRange)": {
10          "[EndTimestamp](API_reader_HLSTimestampRange.md#KinesisVideo-Type-
               reader_HLSTimestampRange-EndTimestamp)": number,
11          "[StartTimestamp](API_reader_HLSTimestampRange.md#KinesisVideo-Type-
               reader_HLSTimestampRange-StartTimestamp)": number
12       }
13    },
14    "[MaxMediaPlaylistFragmentResults](#KinesisVideo-reader_GetHLSStreamingSessionURL-request-
          MaxMediaPlaylistFragmentResults)": number,
15    "[PlaybackMode](#KinesisVideo-reader_GetHLSStreamingSessionURL-request-PlaybackMode)": "
          string",
16    "[StreamARN](#KinesisVideo-reader_GetHLSStreamingSessionURL-request-StreamARN)": "string",
17    "[StreamName](#KinesisVideo-reader_GetHLSStreamingSessionURL-request-StreamName)": "string"
18 }
```

URI Request Parameters

The request does not use any URI parameters.

Request Body

The request accepts the following data in JSON format.

** DiscontinuityMode ** Specifies when flags marking discontinuities between fragments will be added to the media playlists. The default is `ALWAYS` when HLSFragmentSelector is `SERVER_TIMESTAMP`, and `NEVER` when it is `PRODUCER_TIMESTAMP`.
Media players typically build a timeline of media content to play, based on the timestamps of each fragment. This means that if there is any overlap between fragments (as is typical if HLSFragmentSelector is `SERVER_TIMESTAMP`), the media player timeline will have small gaps between fragments in some places, and will overwrite frames in other places. When there are discontinuity flags between fragments, the media player is expected to reset the timeline, resulting in the fragment being played immediately after the previous fragment. We recommend to always have discontinuity flags between fragments if the fragment timestamps are not accurate, or if fragments may be missing. Discontinuity flags should not be placed between fragments for the player timeline to accurately map to the producer timestamps,.
Type: String
Valid Values:`ALWAYS | NEVER`
Required: No

** Expires ** The time in seconds until the requested session expires. This value can be between 300 (5 minutes) and 43200 (12 hours).
When a session expires, no new calls to `GetHLSMasterPlaylist`, `GetHLSMediaPlaylist`, `GetMP4InitFragment`, or `GetMP4MediaFragment` can be made for that session.
The default is 300 (five minutes).
Type: Integer
Valid Range: Minimum value of 300. Maximum value of 43200.
Required: No

** HLSFragmentSelector ** The time range of the requested fragment, and the source of the timestamps.
This parameter is required if `PlaybackMode` is `ON_DEMAND`. This parameter is optional if `PlaybackMode` is `LIVE`. If `PlaybackMode` is `LIVE`, the `FragmentSelectorType` can be set, but the `TimestampRange` should not be set.
Type: HLSFragmentSelector object
Required: No

** MaxMediaPlaylistFragmentResults ** The maximum number of fragments that will be returned in the HLS media playlists.
When the `PlaybackMode` is `LIVE`, the most recent fragments are returned up to this value. When the `PlaybackMode` is `ON_DEMAND`, the oldest fragments are returned, up to this maximum number.
When there are a higher number of fragments available in a live HLS media playlist, video players often buffer content before starting playback. Increasing the buffer size increases the playback latency, but it decreases the likelihood that rebuffering will occur during playback. We recommend that a live HLS media playlist have a minimum of 3 fragments and a maximum of 10 fragments.
The default is 5 fragments if `PlaybackMode` is `LIVE`, and 1000 if `PlaybackMode` is `ON_DEMAND`.
The maximum value of 1000 fragments corresponds to more than 16 minutes of video on streams with one-second fragments, and more than 2 1/2 hours of video on streams with ten-second fragments.
Type: Long
Valid Range: Minimum value of 1. Maximum value of 1000.
Required: No

** PlaybackMode ** Whether to retrieve live or archived, on-demand data.
Features of the two types of session include the following:

- ** LIVE **: For sessions of this type, the HLS media playlist is continually updated with the latest fragments as they become available. We recommend that the media player retrieve a new playlist on a one-second interval. When this type of session is played in a media player, the user interface typically displays a "live" notification, with no scrubber control for choosing the position in the playback window to display. **Note**

  In LIVE mode, the newest available fragments are included in an HLS media playlist, even if there is a gap between fragments (that is, if a fragment is missing). A gap like this might cause a media player to halt or cause a jump in playback. In this mode, fragments are not added to the HLS media playlist if they are older than the newest fragment in the playlist. If the missing fragment becomes available after a subsequent fragment is added to the playlist, the older fragment is not added, and the gap is not filled.

- ** ON_DEMAND **: For sessions of this type, the HLS media playlist contains all the fragments for the session, up to the number that is specified in **MaxMediaPlaylistFragmentResults**. The playlist must be retrieved only once for each session. When this type of session is played in a media player, the user interface typically displays a scrubber control for choosing the position in the playback window to display. In both playback modes, if there are multiple fragments with the same start time stamp, the fragment that has the larger fragment number (that is, the newer fragment) is included in the HLS media playlist. The other fragments are not included. Fragments that have different time stamps but have overlapping durations are still included in the HLS media playlist. This can lead to unexpected behavior in the media player.

  The default is LIVE.

  Type: String

  Valid Values:LIVE | ON_DEMAND

  Required: No

** StreamARN ** The Amazon Resource Name (ARN) of the stream for which to retrieve the HLS master playlist URL.

You must specify either the **StreamName** or the **StreamARN**.

Type: String

Length Constraints: Minimum length of 1. Maximum length of 1024.

Pattern: `arn:aws:kinesisvideo:[a-z0-9-]+:[0-9]+:[a-z]+/[a-zA-Z0-9_.-]+/[0-9]+`

Required: No

** StreamName ** The name of the stream for which to retrieve the HLS master playlist URL.

You must specify either the **StreamName** or the **StreamARN**.

Type: String

Length Constraints: Minimum length of 1. Maximum length of 256.

Pattern: `[a-zA-Z0-9_.-]+`

Required: No

Response Syntax

```
1 HTTP/1.1 200
2 Content-type: application/json
3
4 {
5    "[HLSStreamingSessionURL](#KinesisVideo-reader_GetHLSStreamingSessionURL-response-
        HLSStreamingSessionURL)": "string"
6 }
```

Response Elements

If the action is successful, the service sends back an HTTP 200 response.

The following data is returned in JSON format by the service.

** HLSStreamingSessionURL ** The URL (containing the session token) that a media player can use to retrieve

the HLS master playlist.
Type: String

Errors

For information about the errors that are common to all actions, see Common Errors.

ClientLimitExceededException
Kinesis Video Streams has throttled the request because you have exceeded the limit of allowed client calls. Try making the call later.
HTTP Status Code: 400

InvalidArgumentException
A specified parameter exceeds its restrictions, is not supported, or can't be used.
HTTP Status Code: 400

InvalidCodecPrivateDataException
The Codec Private Data in the video stream is not valid for this operation.
HTTP Status Code: 400

MissingCodecPrivateDataException
No Codec Private Data was found in the video stream.
HTTP Status Code: 400

NoDataRetentionException
A `PlaybackMode` of `ON_DEMAND` was requested for a stream that does not retain data (that is, has a `DataRetentionInHours` of 0).
HTTP Status Code: 400

NotAuthorizedException
Status Code: 403, The caller is not authorized to perform an operation on the given stream, or the token has expired.
HTTP Status Code: 401

ResourceNotFoundException
`GetMedia` throws this error when Kinesis Video Streams can't find the stream that you specified.
`GetHLSStreamingSessionURL` throws this error if a session with a `PlaybackMode` of `ON_DEMAND` is requested for a stream that has no fragments within the requested time range, or if a session with a `PlaybackMode` of `LIVE` is requested for a stream that has no fragments within the last 30 seconds.
HTTP Status Code: 404

UnsupportedStreamMediaTypeException
An HLS streaming session was requested for a stream with a media type that is not `video/h264`.
HTTP Status Code: 400

See Also

For more information about using this API in one of the language-specific AWS SDKs, see the following:

- AWS Command Line Interface
- AWS SDK for .NET
- AWS SDK for C++
- AWS SDK for Go
- AWS SDK for Java
- AWS SDK for JavaScript
- AWS SDK for PHP V3
- AWS SDK for Python

- AWS SDK for Ruby V2

GetMediaForFragmentList

Gets media for a list of fragments (specified by fragment number) from the archived data in an Amazon Kinesis video stream.

The following limits apply when using the GetMediaForFragmentList API:

- A client can call GetMediaForFragmentList up to five times per second per stream.
- Kinesis Video Streams sends media data at a rate of up to 25 megabytes per second (or 200 megabits per second) during a GetMediaForFragmentList session.

Request Syntax

```
1 POST /getMediaForFragmentList HTTP/1.1
2 Content-type: application/json
3
4 {
5    "[Fragments](#KinesisVideo-reader_GetMediaForFragmentList-request-Fragments)": [ "string" ],
6    "[StreamName](#KinesisVideo-reader_GetMediaForFragmentList-request-StreamName)": "string"
7 }
```

URI Request Parameters

The request does not use any URI parameters.

Request Body

The request accepts the following data in JSON format.

** Fragments ** A list of the numbers of fragments for which to retrieve media. You retrieve these values with ListFragments.
Type: Array of strings
Array Members: Minimum number of 1 item. Maximum number of 1000 items.
Length Constraints: Minimum length of 1. Maximum length of 128.
Pattern: ^[0-9]+$
Required: Yes

** StreamName ** The name of the stream from which to retrieve fragment media.
Type: String
Length Constraints: Minimum length of 1. Maximum length of 256.
Pattern: [a-zA-Z0-9_.-]+
Required: Yes

Response Syntax

```
1 HTTP/1.1 200
2 Content-Type: ContentType
3
4 Payload
```

Response Elements

If the action is successful, the service sends back an HTTP 200 response.

The response returns the following HTTP headers.

** ContentType ** The content type of the requested media.
Length Constraints: Minimum length of 1. Maximum length of 128.
Pattern: `^[a-zA-Z0-9_\.\-]+$`

The response returns the following as the HTTP body.

** Payload ** The payload that Kinesis Video Streams returns is a sequence of chunks from the specified stream. For information about the chunks, see PutMedia. The chunks that Kinesis Video Streams returns in the `GetMediaForFragmentList` call also include the following additional Matroska (MKV) tags:

- AWS_KINESISVIDEO_FRAGMENT_NUMBER - Fragment number returned in the chunk.
- AWS_KINESISVIDEO_SERVER_SIDE_TIMESTAMP - Server-side time stamp of the fragment.
- AWS_KINESISVIDEO_PRODUCER_SIDE_TIMESTAMP - Producer-side time stamp of the fragment. The following tags will be included if an exception occurs:
- AWS_KINESISVIDEO_FRAGMENT_NUMBER - The number of the fragment that threw the exception
- AWS_KINESISVIDEO_EXCEPTION_ERROR_CODE - The integer code of the exception
- AWS_KINESISVIDEO_EXCEPTION_MESSAGE - A text description of the exception

Errors

For information about the errors that are common to all actions, see Common Errors.

ClientLimitExceededException
Kinesis Video Streams has throttled the request because you have exceeded the limit of allowed client calls. Try making the call later.
HTTP Status Code: 400

InvalidArgumentException
A specified parameter exceeds its restrictions, is not supported, or can't be used.
HTTP Status Code: 400

NotAuthorizedException
Status Code: 403, The caller is not authorized to perform an operation on the given stream, or the token has expired.
HTTP Status Code: 401

ResourceNotFoundException
`GetMedia` throws this error when Kinesis Video Streams can't find the stream that you specified.
`GetHLSStreamingSessionURL` throws this error if a session with a `PlaybackMode` of `ON_DEMAND` is requested for a stream that has no fragments within the requested time range, or if a session with a `PlaybackMode` of `LIVE` is requested for a stream that has no fragments within the last 30 seconds.
HTTP Status Code: 404

See Also

For more information about using this API in one of the language-specific AWS SDKs, see the following:

- AWS Command Line Interface
- AWS SDK for .NET
- AWS SDK for C++
- AWS SDK for Go
- AWS SDK for Java
- AWS SDK for JavaScript
- AWS SDK for PHP V3
- AWS SDK for Python

- AWS SDK for Ruby V2

ListFragments

Returns a list of Fragment objects from the specified stream and start location within the archived data.

Request Syntax

```
1  POST /listFragments HTTP/1.1
2  Content-type: application/json
3
4  {
5      "[FragmentSelector](#KinesisVideo-reader_ListFragments-request-FragmentSelector)": {
6          "[FragmentSelectorType](API_reader_FragmentSelector.md#KinesisVideo-Type-
               reader_FragmentSelector-FragmentSelectorType)": "string",
7          "[TimestampRange](API_reader_FragmentSelector.md#KinesisVideo-Type-reader_FragmentSelector
               -TimestampRange)": {
8              "[EndTimestamp](API_reader_TimestampRange.md#KinesisVideo-Type-reader_TimestampRange-
                   EndTimestamp)": number,
9              "[StartTimestamp](API_reader_TimestampRange.md#KinesisVideo-Type-reader_TimestampRange-
                   StartTimestamp)": number
10         }
11     },
12     "[MaxResults](#KinesisVideo-reader_ListFragments-request-MaxResults)": number,
13     "[NextToken](#KinesisVideo-reader_ListFragments-request-NextToken)": "string",
14     "[StreamName](#KinesisVideo-reader_ListFragments-request-StreamName)": "string"
15 }
```

URI Request Parameters

The request does not use any URI parameters.

Request Body

The request accepts the following data in JSON format.

** FragmentSelector ** Describes the time stamp range and time stamp origin for the range of fragments to return.
Type: FragmentSelector object
Required: No

** MaxResults ** The total number of fragments to return. If the total number of fragments available is more than the value specified in `max-results`, then a ListFragments:NextToken is provided in the output that you can use to resume pagination.
Type: Long
Valid Range: Minimum value of 1. Maximum value of 1000.
Required: No

** NextToken ** A token to specify where to start paginating. This is the ListFragments:NextToken from a previously truncated response.
Type: String
Length Constraints: Minimum length of 1.
Required: No

** StreamName ** The name of the stream from which to retrieve a fragment list.
Type: String

Length Constraints: Minimum length of 1. Maximum length of 256.
Pattern: [a-zA-Z0-9_.-]+
Required: Yes

Response Syntax

```
1  HTTP/1.1 200
2  Content-type: application/json
3
4  {
5    "[Fragments](#KinesisVideo-reader_ListFragments-response-Fragments)": [
6      {
7        "[FragmentLengthInMilliseconds](API_reader_Fragment.md#KinesisVideo-Type-
           reader_Fragment-FragmentLengthInMilliseconds)": number,
8        "[FragmentNumber](API_reader_Fragment.md#KinesisVideo-Type-reader_Fragment-
           FragmentNumber)": "string",
9        "[FragmentSizeInBytes](API_reader_Fragment.md#KinesisVideo-Type-reader_Fragment-
           FragmentSizeInBytes)": number,
10       "[ProducerTimestamp](API_reader_Fragment.md#KinesisVideo-Type-reader_Fragment-
           ProducerTimestamp)": number,
11       "[ServerTimestamp](API_reader_Fragment.md#KinesisVideo-Type-reader_Fragment-
           ServerTimestamp)": number
12     }
13   ],
14   "[NextToken](#KinesisVideo-reader_ListFragments-response-NextToken)": "string"
15 }
```

Response Elements

If the action is successful, the service sends back an HTTP 200 response.

The following data is returned in JSON format by the service.

** Fragments ** A list of fragment numbers that correspond to the time stamp range provided.
Type: Array of Fragment objects

** NextToken ** If the returned list is truncated, the operation returns this token to use to retrieve the next page of results. This value is null when there are no more results to return.
Type: String
Length Constraints: Minimum length of 1.

Errors

For information about the errors that are common to all actions, see Common Errors.

ClientLimitExceededException
Kinesis Video Streams has throttled the request because you have exceeded the limit of allowed client calls. Try making the call later.
HTTP Status Code: 400

InvalidArgumentException
A specified parameter exceeds its restrictions, is not supported, or can't be used.
HTTP Status Code: 400

NotAuthorizedException
Status Code: 403, The caller is not authorized to perform an operation on the given stream, or the token has

expired.
HTTP Status Code: 401

ResourceNotFoundException
GetMedia throws this error when Kinesis Video Streams can't find the stream that you specified.
GetHLSStreamingSessionURL throws this error if a session with a PlaybackMode of ON_DEMAND is requested for
a stream that has no fragments within the requested time range, or if a session with a PlaybackMode of LIVE is
requested for a stream that has no fragments within the last 30 seconds.
HTTP Status Code: 404

See Also

For more information about using this API in one of the language-specific AWS SDKs, see the following:

- AWS Command Line Interface
- AWS SDK for .NET
- AWS SDK for C++
- AWS SDK for Go
- AWS SDK for Java
- AWS SDK for JavaScript
- AWS SDK for PHP V3
- AWS SDK for Python
- AWS SDK for Ruby V2

Data Types

The following data types are supported by Amazon Kinesis Video Streams:

- StreamInfo
- StreamNameCondition

The following data types are supported by Amazon Kinesis Video Streams Media:

- StartSelector

The following data types are supported by Amazon Kinesis Video Streams Archived Media:

- Fragment
- FragmentSelector
- HLSFragmentSelector
- HLSTimestampRange
- TimestampRange

StreamInfo

An object describing a Kinesis video stream.

Contents

CreationTime A time stamp that indicates when the stream was created.
Type: Timestamp
Required: No

DataRetentionInHours How long the stream retains data, in hours.
Type: Integer
Valid Range: Minimum value of 0.
Required: No

DeviceName The name of the device that is associated with the stream.
Type: String
Length Constraints: Minimum length of 1. Maximum length of 128.
Pattern: `[a-zA-Z0-9_.-]+`
Required: No

KmsKeyId The ID of the AWS Key Management Service (AWS KMS) key that Kinesis Video Streams uses to encrypt data on the stream.
Type: String
Length Constraints: Minimum length of 1. Maximum length of 2048.
Required: No

MediaType The `MediaType` of the stream.
Type: String
Length Constraints: Minimum length of 1. Maximum length of 128.
Pattern: `[\w\-\.\+]+/[\w\-\.\+]+`
Required: No

Status The status of the stream.
Type: String
Valid Values:`CREATING | ACTIVE | UPDATING | DELETING`
Required: No

StreamARN The Amazon Resource Name (ARN) of the stream.
Type: String
Length Constraints: Minimum length of 1. Maximum length of 1024.
Pattern: `arn:aws:kinesisvideo:[a-z0-9-]+:[0-9]+:[a-z]+/[a-zA-Z0-9_.-]+/[0-9]+`
Required: No

StreamName The name of the stream.
Type: String
Length Constraints: Minimum length of 1. Maximum length of 256.
Pattern: `[a-zA-Z0-9_.-]+`
Required: No

Version The version of the stream.
Type: String
Length Constraints: Minimum length of 1. Maximum length of 64.
Pattern: `[a-zA-Z0-9]+`
Required: No

See Also

For more information about using this API in one of the language-specific AWS SDKs, see the following:

- AWS SDK for C++
- AWS SDK for Go
- AWS SDK for Java
- AWS SDK for Ruby V2

StreamNameCondition

Specifies the condition that streams must satisfy to be returned when you list streams (see the `ListStreams` API). A condition has a comparison operation and a value. Currently, you can specify only the `BEGINS_WITH` operator, which finds streams whose names start with a given prefix.

Contents

ComparisonOperator A comparison operator. Currently, you can specify only the `BEGINS_WITH` operator, which finds streams whose names start with a given prefix.
Type: String
Valid Values:`BEGINS_WITH`
Required: No

ComparisonValue A value to compare.
Type: String
Length Constraints: Minimum length of 1. Maximum length of 256.
Pattern: `[a-zA-Z0-9_.-]+`
Required: No

See Also

For more information about using this API in one of the language-specific AWS SDKs, see the following:

- AWS SDK for C++
- AWS SDK for Go
- AWS SDK for Java
- AWS SDK for Ruby V2

StartSelector

Identifies the chunk on the Kinesis video stream where you want the `GetMedia` API to start returning media data. You have the following options to identify the starting chunk:

- Choose the latest (or oldest) chunk.
- Identify a specific chunk. You can identify a specific chunk either by providing a fragment number or time stamp (server or producer).
- Each chunk's metadata includes a continuation token as a Matroska (MKV) tag (`AWS_KINESISVIDEO_CONTINUATION_TOKEN`). If your previous `GetMedia` request terminated, you can use this tag value in your next `GetMedia` request. The API then starts returning chunks starting where the last API ended.

Contents

AfterFragmentNumber Specifies the fragment number from where you want the `GetMedia` API to start returning the fragments.
Type: String
Length Constraints: Minimum length of 1. Maximum length of 128.
Pattern: `^[0-9]+$`
Required: No

ContinuationToken Continuation token that Kinesis Video Streams returned in the previous `GetMedia` response. The `GetMedia` API then starts with the chunk identified by the continuation token.
Type: String
Length Constraints: Minimum length of 1. Maximum length of 128.
Pattern: `^[a-zA-Z0-9_\.\-]+$`
Required: No

StartSelectorType Identifies the fragment on the Kinesis video stream where you want to start getting the data from.

- NOW - Start with the latest chunk on the stream.
- EARLIEST - Start with earliest available chunk on the stream.
- FRAGMENT_NUMBER - Start with the chunk containing the specific fragment. You must also specify the `StartFragmentNumber`.
- PRODUCER_TIMESTAMP or SERVER_TIMESTAMP - Start with the chunk containing a fragment with the specified producer or server time stamp. You specify the time stamp by adding `StartTimestamp`.
- CONTINUATION_TOKEN - Read using the specified continuation token. If you choose the NOW, EARLIEST, or CONTINUATION_TOKEN as the `startSelectorType`, you don't provide any additional information in the `startSelector`. Type: String
  Valid Values:`FRAGMENT_NUMBER | SERVER_TIMESTAMP | PRODUCER_TIMESTAMP | NOW | EARLIEST | CONTINUATION_TOKEN`
  Required: Yes

StartTimestamp A time stamp value. This value is required if you choose the PRODUCER_TIMESTAMP or the SERVER_TIMESTAMP as the `startSelectorType`. The `GetMedia` API then starts with the chunk containing the fragment that has the specified time stamp.
Type: Timestamp
Required: No

See Also

For more information about using this API in one of the language-specific AWS SDKs, see the following:

- AWS SDK for C++
- AWS SDK for Go
- AWS SDK for Java
- AWS SDK for Ruby V2

Fragment

Represents a segment of video or other time-delimited data.

Contents

FragmentLengthInMilliseconds The playback duration or other time value associated with the fragment.
Type: Long
Required: No

FragmentNumber The index value of the fragment.
Type: String
Length Constraints: Minimum length of 1.
Required: No

FragmentSizeInBytes The total fragment size, including information about the fragment and contained media data.
Type: Long
Required: No

ProducerTimestamp The time stamp from the producer corresponding to the fragment.
Type: Timestamp
Required: No

ServerTimestamp The time stamp from the AWS server corresponding to the fragment.
Type: Timestamp
Required: No

See Also

For more information about using this API in one of the language-specific AWS SDKs, see the following:
- AWS SDK for C++
- AWS SDK for Go
- AWS SDK for Java
- AWS SDK for Ruby V2

FragmentSelector

Describes the time stamp range and time stamp origin of a range of fragments.

Contents

FragmentSelectorType The origin of the time stamps to use (Server or Producer).
Type: String
Valid Values:PRODUCER_TIMESTAMP | SERVER_TIMESTAMP
Required: Yes

TimestampRange The range of time stamps to return.
Type: TimestampRange object
Required: Yes

See Also

For more information about using this API in one of the language-specific AWS SDKs, see the following:

- AWS SDK for C++
- AWS SDK for Go
- AWS SDK for Java
- AWS SDK for Ruby V2

HLSFragmentSelector

Contains the range of time stamps for the requested media, and the source of the time stamps.

Contents

FragmentSelectorType The source of the time stamps for the requested media.
When `FragmentSelectorType` is set to `PRODUCER_TIMESTAMP`, and GetHLSStreamingSessionURL:PlaybackMode is `ON_DEMAND`, the first fragment ingested with a producer timestamp within the specified FragmentSelector:TimestampRange will be included in the media playlist. In addition, the fragments with producer timestamps within the `TimestampRange` ingested immediately following the first fragment (up to the GetHLSStreamingSessionURL:MaxMediaPlaylistFragmentResults value) will also be included. Fragments with duplicate producer timestamps will be deduplicated. This means that if producers are producing a stream of fragments with producer timestamps that are approximately equal to the true clock time, then the HLS media playlists will contain all of the fragments within the requested time stamp range. If some fragments are ingested within the same time range and very different points in time, only the oldest ingested collection of fragments will be returned.
When `FragmentSelectorType` is set to `PRODUCER_TIMESTAMP`, and GetHLSStreamingSessionURL:PlaybackMode is `LIVE`, the producer timestamps will be used in the MP4 fragments and for deduplication, but the most recently ingested fragments based on server timestamps will be included in the HLS media playlist. This means that even if fragments ingested in the past have producer timestamps with values now, they will not be included in the HLS media playlist.
The default is `SERVER_TIMESTAMP`.
Type: String
Valid Values:`PRODUCER_TIMESTAMP` | `SERVER_TIMESTAMP`
Required: No

TimestampRange The start and end of the time stamp range for the requested media.
This value should not be present if `PlaybackType` is `LIVE`.
Type: HLSTimestampRange object
Required: No

See Also

For more information about using this API in one of the language-specific AWS SDKs, see the following:

- AWS SDK for C++
- AWS SDK for Go
- AWS SDK for Java
- AWS SDK for Ruby V2

HLSTimestampRange

The start and end of the time stamp range for the requested media.

This value should not be present if `PlaybackType` is `LIVE`.

Note
The values in the `HLSTimestampRange` are inclusive. Fragments that begin before the start time but continue past it, or fragments that begin before the end time but continue past it, are included in the session.

Contents

EndTimestamp The end of the time stamp range for the requested media. This value must be within three hours of the specified `StartTimestamp`, and it must be later than the `StartTimestamp` value.
If `FragmentSelectorType` for the request is `SERVER_TIMESTAMP`, this value must be in the past.
If the `HLSTimestampRange` value is specified, the `EndTimestamp` value is required.
This value is inclusive. The `EndTimestamp` is compared to the (starting) time stamp of the fragment. Fragments that start before the `EndTimestamp` value and continue past it are included in the session. Type: Timestamp
Required: No

StartTimestamp The start of the time stamp range for the requested media.
If the `HLSTimestampRange` value is specified, the `StartTimestamp` value is required.
This value is inclusive. Fragments that start before the `StartingTimestamp` and continue past it are included in the session. Type: Timestamp
Required: No

See Also

For more information about using this API in one of the language-specific AWS SDKs, see the following:

- AWS SDK for C++
- AWS SDK for Go
- AWS SDK for Java
- AWS SDK for Ruby V2

TimestampRange

The range of time stamps for which to return fragments.

Contents

EndTimestamp The ending time stamp in the range of time stamps for which to return fragments.
Type: Timestamp
Required: Yes

StartTimestamp The starting time stamp in the range of time stamps for which to return fragments.
Type: Timestamp
Required: Yes

See Also

For more information about using this API in one of the language-specific AWS SDKs, see the following:

- AWS SDK for C++
- AWS SDK for Go
- AWS SDK for Java
- AWS SDK for Ruby V2

Common Errors

This section lists the errors common to the API actions of all AWS services. For errors specific to an API action for this service, see the topic for that API action.

AccessDeniedException
You do not have sufficient access to perform this action.
HTTP Status Code: 400

IncompleteSignature
The request signature does not conform to AWS standards.
HTTP Status Code: 400

InternalFailure The request processing has failed because of an unknown error, exception or failure.
HTTP Status Code: 500

InvalidAction The action or operation requested is invalid. Verify that the action is typed correctly.
HTTP Status Code: 400

InvalidClientTokenId The X.509 certificate or AWS access key ID provided does not exist in our records.
HTTP Status Code: 403

InvalidParameterCombination Parameters that must not be used together were used together.
HTTP Status Code: 400

InvalidParameterValue An invalid or out-of-range value was supplied for the input parameter.
HTTP Status Code: 400

InvalidQueryParameter The AWS query string is malformed or does not adhere to AWS standards.
HTTP Status Code: 400

MalformedQueryString The query string contains a syntax error.
HTTP Status Code: 404

MissingAction The request is missing an action or a required parameter.
HTTP Status Code: 400

MissingAuthenticationToken The request must contain either a valid (registered) AWS access key ID or X.509 certificate.
HTTP Status Code: 403

MissingParameter A required parameter for the specified action is not supplied.
HTTP Status Code: 400

OptInRequired The AWS access key ID needs a subscription for the service.
HTTP Status Code: 403

RequestExpired The request reached the service more than 15 minutes after the date stamp on the request or more than 15 minutes after the request expiration date (such as for pre-signed URLs), or the date stamp on the request is more than 15 minutes in the future.
HTTP Status Code: 400

ServiceUnavailable The request has failed due to a temporary failure of the server.
HTTP Status Code: 503

ThrottlingException The request was denied due to request throttling.
HTTP Status Code: 400

ValidationError The input fails to satisfy the constraints specified by an AWS service.
HTTP Status Code: 400

Common Parameters

The following list contains the parameters that all actions use for signing Signature Version 4 requests with a query string. Any action-specific parameters are listed in the topic for that action. For more information about Signature Version 4, see Signature Version 4 Signing Process in the *Amazon Web Services General Reference*.

Action The action to be performed.
Type: string
Required: Yes

Version The API version that the request is written for, expressed in the format YYYY-MM-DD.
Type: string
Required: Yes

X-Amz-Algorithm The hash algorithm that you used to create the request signature.
Condition: Specify this parameter when you include authentication information in a query string instead of in the HTTP authorization header.
Type: string
Valid Values: `AWS4-HMAC-SHA256`
Required: Conditional

X-Amz-Credential The credential scope value, which is a string that includes your access key, the date, the region you are targeting, the service you are requesting, and a termination string ("aws4_request"). The value is expressed in the following format: *access_key/YYYYMMDD/region/service*/aws4_request.
For more information, see Task 2: Create a String to Sign for Signature Version 4 in the *Amazon Web Services General Reference*.
Condition: Specify this parameter when you include authentication information in a query string instead of in the HTTP authorization header.
Type: string
Required: Conditional

X-Amz-Date The date that is used to create the signature. The format must be ISO 8601 basic format (YYYYMMDD'T'HHMMSS'Z'). For example, the following date time is a valid X-Amz-Date value: `20120325 T120000Z`.
Condition: X-Amz-Date is optional for all requests; it can be used to override the date used for signing requests. If the Date header is specified in the ISO 8601 basic format, X-Amz-Date is not required. When X-Amz-Date is used, it always overrides the value of the Date header. For more information, see Handling Dates in Signature Version 4 in the *Amazon Web Services General Reference*.
Type: string
Required: Conditional

X-Amz-Security-Token The temporary security token that was obtained through a call to AWS Security Token Service (AWS STS). For a list of services that support temporary security credentials from AWS Security Token Service, go to AWS Services That Work with IAM in the *IAM User Guide*.
Condition: If you're using temporary security credentials from the AWS Security Token Service, you must include the security token.
Type: string
Required: Conditional

X-Amz-Signature Specifies the hex-encoded signature that was calculated from the string to sign and the derived signing key.
Condition: Specify this parameter when you include authentication information in a query string instead of in the HTTP authorization header.
Type: string
Required: Conditional

X-Amz-SignedHeaders Specifies all the HTTP headers that were included as part of the canonical request. For more information about specifying signed headers, see Task 1: Create a Canonical Request For Signature

Version 4 in the * Amazon Web Services General Reference*.
Condition: Specify this parameter when you include authentication information in a query string instead of in the HTTP authorization header.
Type: string
Required: Conditional

www.ingramcontent.com/pod-product-compliance
Lightning Source LLC
LaVergne TN
LVHW082038050326
832904LV00005B/227